WOUNDS TO WISDOM

9 STORIES GUIDING YOU TO ALCHEMIZE YOUR PAIN INTO YOUR GREATEST GIFT

ANASTASIA VIRGINILLO   CHEYENNE LINDEMUTH

DOROTHY KNIGHT   DR. FALAK SHAIKH   IRMA PAREDES

LYSA GYLEN   RACHEL ANNE WATKINS

TINA SIMONE MOWATT REECE   VALERIE SMITH

SOULFULLY ALIGNED PUBLISHING HOUSE

This book and its proceedings are dedicated to the Shwas Organization of India, whose mission is to provide resources and opportunities for education to underprivileged kids.

Education in its purest sense is expanding the horizon of human perception. But we see some of the nation's toughest challenges: Teacher-student ratio, Infrastructure, Cultural background, and Poverty. All of these result in no pre-primary education, weak academic foundation and maximum dropout ratio at 8th and 10th grade, which forces the students to pursue the labour work that their parents are doing.

Shwas aims at providing a safe and healthy environment to children so that they can openly share with them the challenges they face that holds them back from aspiring their dreams.

We truly believe what Maria Montessori had said, "Education of even a small child, therefore, does not aim at preparing for school, but preparing him for life."

We feel blessed to support the cause that "SHWAS" stands for.

Thank you SHWAS for making a difference!!!

CONTENTS

INTRODUCTION

What is in the past, no longer matters. Learning how to shift and alchemise what no longer serves us is a gift. Together we rise, creating a new paradigm shift, for you, for me, and for us!

Many of us experience emotional wounds as a child. Perhaps one of your parents or caregivers withdrew from you emotionally or physically. Or perhaps they were too controlling or harshly criticised you, making you feel guilty for being your true self. Maybe you were physically abused, ridiculed, humiliated, or neglected, and not appreciated for who you were. Maybe you were judged harshly, and now you feel inadequate about yourself. As a result of these and other incidents that came from other family members, you took on a childhood wound, negative beliefs about yourself, and believed that you are not lovable.

When a mother fails to meet the needs of a child to provide love, care, and nurturing, or is abusive, absent, or wounded herself, this leads to the wound in the child, often called the mother wound. The attachment theory by psychologist Mary Ainsworth talks about how the trust that a mother instils in childhood will have a positive impact on a child's future and their relationships. This means that a wounded child will most likely have a similar relationship with her/his children.

The same goes with the father wound. When a father fails to fulfil the needs of a child by failing to provide, protect, or establish security, it creates a wound for the child. These wounds are passed on from generation to generation. As children grow up, they live their life through the painted glass of these patterns created by these wounds.

Often these woundings can be ancestral or generational which are stored in the tissue, cells, and DNA as an imprint. They live through the person who is carrying them, just to be passed on to the next generation as an inheritance.

Unresolved wounds create physical, mental, and emotional pain. They damage our relationships, negatively impact our careers, and often end up in self-destructive behaviour. The unresolved issue becomes part of our identity, and we subconsciously remain angry, resentful, hold on to grudges, and often create self-sabotaging patterns and we do not know why.

These wounds stay hidden in our subconscious and unconscious and drive our life until we take responsibility for their healing.

THE WOUND IS NOT YOUR FAULT,
BUT HEALING IS YOUR RESPONSIBILITY
~Denice Frohman

Each wound brings wisdom with itself. When we acknowledge the wound we face it, resolve, and heal it. We forgive those who have caused it, and we can integrate the wisdom it has for us.

When these wounds remain unhealed, the same patterns, and the same stories will be playing up over and over in our lives and you will be wondering why you keep being stuck in a loop. These patterns and stories are passed on to the generations to come after you.

When you start working on yourself by doing inner work and healing wounds, a vibrational frequency shift occurs. Your consciousness will shift as will your energy field. Once you shift your vibration, everything around you changes for good in each area of your life.

And now that you are free from your story, you can see things from a different perspective. Even if you revisit your story, you are not limited or constricted in any way by it, but now you can see the lessons and wisdom it has brought to you. It changes your whole perspective on life itself. Your life becomes a masterpiece.

And this is how it all shifted for us. Nine women from across the globe came together to share our personal, heartfelt stories of healing, transforming, and alchemising our deep-rooted wounds into wisdom. Our intentions in writing this book are to share the lessons we have learnt on our journey, whilst healing the wounds and integrating wisdom in our lives to assist and inspire you to face your wounds and bring in healing.

By reading our stories, you may find some answers you've been looking for, and you may look at your life journey and discover your own unique codes that you would like to share with humanity.

May this book offer you a solution, guidance, and a paradigm shift on your journey of self-actualisation and empowerment.

Our wish for you is to look at your wounds with compassion. Love them, do not run away from them, feel them to heal them, and see them dissolve.

Your spirit is strong, and you can turn challenges into opportunities. Let us show you how!

~ Lysa Gylen and Dr Falak Shaikh

∼

One day, you will heal

One day, you will be grateful for the deepest cuts of pain
One day, you will glance at yourself
And see a stronger person through your reflection
One day, you will kiss away your hurt... gently, and with grace
Until then, use it all to propel you forward
Like a white-hot pyre through your star-spangled eyes
A fire to regenerate every shadowy cell
And open your heart to every experience
Knowing that one day
You will search your heart
And understand that love is the only thing to ever hold onto.

~ "One Day" from Beating Hearts and Butterflies

ANASTASIA VIRGINILLO

BECOMING HER: CONFESSIONS OF A VALIDATION ADDICT

To all the little girls who don't feel whole and complete just the way you are,
"I mean you no harm but may the best disasters come to you." (Smith, Dan. 'Good News First', 2017.)

FIGHTS AND FEELINGS

*S*itting on the top step in our fuzzy onesie pajamas, we could hear the angry voices echoing up the stairs from the kitchen below. I remember my tired mind thinking it would be a long while before we got to sleep. It always was a long night when they fought. Turning to Sammy, and with all the assertiveness I could muster in my five-year-old body, I told my little sister to go back to bed. Her anticipated refusal came swiftly, and I knew what we had to do next. My desire to protect her was surpassed by the magnetic pull for the two of us to go downstairs and "fix the problem", so on we went.

Despite the slew of failed attempts we always tried, hopelessly optimistic, that mom and dad would stop fighting, hug each other, hug us, and we could all finally go to sleep. Crawling backwards down the stairs as silently as possible I felt the air become cold and stale. It was as if the safe and secure home from earlier that day was replaced by an exact but empty replica. It looked like home, but it did not feel like home anymore. The words of resentment sliced through the air sticking to the skin on the back of my neck and sending chills through my body. And yet, despite the danger I felt, the draw to be closer persisted. Turning the corner, hand in hand (I always made Sammy hold my hand), we saw them at the kitchen table, the space that would eventually become our family's boxing ring. There they were, in their usual fighting stances, throwing words like haymakers through the air.

We injected ourselves into the kitchen with the desperate hope that they would see us and be embarrassed enough to stop, but they never did. Mom was always the first to say, "Go back to bed!" and although in that house her word was law, the laws were blurred when the adults were occupied in their own painful wounding. So we stayed. Never understanding what the fight was about, never knowing what we could do to make it all better. That was the most frustrating part, we could *never make it better.*

Our home didn't quite feel whole. And in those rare moments when it did, there was a looming knowing that it could be taken away at any time. These nights always ended the same. Dad would storm off, mom often chasing him, and Sammy and I, with our fuzzy-footed pajamas, would be left standing on the porch, feeling completely and utterly helpless.

Eventually, mom would come back, tuck us into bed, and wait up all night long for dad to come home. I'm grateful to say that even to this day, he *always* comes home.

Even though the battle was over, it never quite felt complete. I remember on more than one occasion laying in bed as the chills dissipated from my body, leaving a feeling of emptiness in its wake. I needed to grow up faster. *"If I was just bigger, older, and smarter, I could help. I could make them stop fighting."* I deeply believed that if I could just understand the problem, I could create the solution.

From before I can remember, I've attempted to impact the environment around me to feel safe and secure. I felt it was my responsibility to keep the peace, and my obligation to comply with the forces around me. In order to gain the knowledge I needed to fix the problems in life, I chose to live in pursuit of understanding people, how they communicated, and how they related to one another. I feared that without my efforts, I would forever be a helpless victim. This began a life of exchanging my own needs and desires for what I believed others needed to see. By choosing to create as little disharmony as possible in this world, becoming the "good girl" seemed like my only option.

THE 'GOOD GIRL'

I reluctantly entered the classroom, hoping I had walked slowly enough to miss the conversation that was happening. When I appeared in the doorway, each and every set of beady fifth grade eyes were on me. I made sure not to make eye contact and quickly took a seat as far back from everyone as I could. And that's when my teacher started to speak, "I have heard many of you teasing another student about being a teacher's pet..." As those judgmental beady eyes found their way back to me again, my whole body tensed up, and I could feel the heat of embarrassment radiating from my face. Had she not warned me earlier, I may have tried to convince myself that she was talking about someone else, that my friends would never say that about me, and that I was in fact 'safe' in not being singled out as the class kiss-ass. "It's important for us to be respectful of those in the classroom and understand that...", she went on, but I wasn't listening. No one was. I could see from the periphery of my vision that they were instead watching me, though I didn't dare lift my head to confirm. It was all I could do to stifle the tears that desperately wanted to fall from my mortified face. I wanted to run, but out of fear of making an even bigger scene, I stayed, beet red and utterly imprisoned by my feelings.

I was the kind of kid who received great joy from doing well in school. I wasn't the smartest or the most gifted student, but my obedience was consistently praised by teachers. I took this form of validation to mean that I was doing the right thing. Dad always said, "the greatest failure of life is the failure to follow instructions," and in my attempt to be a 'good girl' I made sure to always follow those instructions, do as I was told, and not create problems.

I may not have been the smartest in the class but I was smart enough to know that I was definitely a teacher's pet. I just didn't know that *they* all knew. That *they* talked about it out of earshot. That *they*, my only friends, were the ones making fun of me enough to warrant this humiliating conversation. At merely ten years old, this was my worst nightmare. "They hate me," I confirmed. "They all hate me, nowhere is safe, and there's nothing I can do about it."

Despite my efforts, there always seemed to be incalculable challenges within the complex landscape of growing up. In an attempt to not say or do anything that would be upsetting to the authority figures in my life, I left myself vulnerable to my peers which invited that feeling of helpless emptiness back into my heart.

If acceptance satisfied me, disapproval terrified me. So as we returned to our seats for our regularly scheduled English lesson, I realized that just being a good girl wasn't going to cut it anymore. If I was going to prevent that embarrassing mishap from ever happening again, I would need to get better at controlling the way other people perceived me.

So I did.

Just like you probably don't remember how you started walking, I don't remember when I started mirroring the actions and behaviours of others to gain their approval. I don't remember when I started lying to create fabricated bonds of similarities so that others would feel comfortable around me. And I don't remember when it started to inform each and every interaction of my life. But it did. I became a master manipulative communicator, learning how to tell the truth, the half truth, and nothing close to the truth in order to hide the perceived bad, and highlight the perceived good of who I was. I became proficient at changing my colours on command.

In elementary school, I would gossip with the cool kids while playing Harriet the Spy with the nerdy ones. In middle school, I made friends with anyone I could while maintaining the good grades needed for praise and approval from my parents and teachers. In high school, I alternated between hanging out at the smokestack and in the library.

I started seeking signs of affection in every interaction as a checkpoint to let me know that I was in someone's good graces. I became hyper aware and sensitive to subtle shifts in demeanor so I could notice any indication that my likeability rankings may be going down. Like a chameleon, I morphed my mannerisms, body language, tone of voice, and even my clothing so others would see me as 'just like them' and therefore worth keeping around. By university, I was confident in my ability to make friends with pretty much anyone.

As I got better at mirroring others, the validation came pouring in and I was intoxicated by it. I lived for the compliments, praise, and reassurance my friends gave me. It really pays to be a 'good girl'. With many sources to draw from, I revelled in the safety and security that it brought me. As far as I could tell, it was working.

Here's the thing with external validation: no matter how much you have, it'll always leave you wanting more.

As expected, I found someone who would give me just that

JAY

Falling in love with Jay was the easiest thing I ever did. He was smart, mysterious, and perfectly articulate. His ability to communicate profound thoughts and complex feelings captivated my attention and I instantly felt safe and at home in his arms. Receiving his love was exhilarating and deeply satisfying making it only a matter of time before he became my consistent and reliable source of affection.

From this point forward, love became my drug of choice.

I poured my soul into that man and relished in the joy of watching him turn it into beautiful words I could not speak, and music I could not play. The reflection of who I was, and who he saw me as, was returned tenfold with a radiant sparkle I had never seen before. He was my willing addiction.

He played a mean guitar and sang songs like Layla by Eric Clapton, and Black by Pearl Jam as if they were written for me. I felt depth in our connection, and a sense of completeness that always escaped me. Clearly, I was hooked.

I saw parts of myself that I loved for the first time through his eyes. He taught me how to feel; how to melt into the joy of being high and naked listening to Red Hot Chili Peppers until all hours of the night. His love uncovered the woman I wanted to be because he saw me as HER already; strong, bold, articulate, and wildly playful.

With him I felt secure, settled, and whole. There was nothing for me to fix. There was only peace, and I willingly melted in its comfort.

As seems standard for young couples, we acted as though our love was the answer to all of life's problems. And for a good long time, it was. I found solace in his steady embrace when in the darkness of perpetual family arguments, and he did the same during the death of his big hearted dad. I can admit now that we were codependent.

When life got challenging, I wasn't getting the fix I needed. My wandering eye wanted more. Another hit. Another source. A new strain of my beloved's validation to fill the returning emptiness I felt inside.

And so, on I went.

ZED

You know that feeling you got as a kid the day before you were about to leave for vacation? That giddy anticipation? That was Zed. He was my fairytale love away from home while I was in Florida for an internship at Disney World. Ironically, this was the perfect place for a smiley, people-pleasing, good girl to hide in plain sight. I fit right in.

This man was a dream. He opened doors for strangers, pulled over to help others stuck on the side of the road, and never forgot to grab food to feed the homeless man and his dog across the street. Even when that dog bit him in the face, he blamed himself and compassionately understood the pup's attempt to protect its owner. *What a guy!*

My heart was his from day one, and it would be years before I ever fully got it back.

I wanted to never look away from him. For us to exist in the perfect moments of bliss between heartbeats. His love illuminated a version of myself I had only ever dreamt of being. He saw me as wildly confident, resilient, courageous, and above all else, adventurous. The more time I spent with him, the more he pulled HER out of me. Dancing in the kitchen to Louis Armstrong was all I thought I would ever need to feel truly whole in this world.

He was my fairytale love.

My one and done love.

My "This Is Us" love.

My proposal under a waterfall with a blade of grass for a ring love.

So of course, when my internship ended, we decided to do long-distance.

I felt I had all I needed. If I had him and some trees to climb for the rest of my life, I would be happy. And in all honesty, if we remained in proximity to one another, that may very well have been true.

I wanted to get clean. I wanted his love to be the only love I ever needed but I was also scared. I didn't trust that I could do it. I didn't trust *myself*.

Distance is dangerous for a validation addict in denial, and so, our epic love story would inevitably end in disaster.

DISASTER

With my heart in another country, I returned to Toronto, reluctantly, going through the motions of settling into a home that felt unfamiliar, while secretly plotting my escape back to Zed.

Within months, there was no safe place. My life was upside down and I found myself again, homeless at heart.

My friends had all left our university town where I lived, the new job was a dud, mom and dad were unsupportive of my life choices, and worst of all, Zed was emotionally withdrawing. His job as a firefighter had him working 24-48 hour shifts so after a few long nights and bad calls, he needed space and replenishment, of which I had nothing to offer him.

You can't give from an empty cup. And when your cup is always being filled by others, you'll find yourself staring at the bottom of your mug more often than not.

I was broken again, feeling empty on the inside, pretending everything was okay on the outside. I tried to convince my parents that the new job was working out and that I was doing well. I just wanted them to be proud of me. I also attempted to reassure Zed that I was adjusting to the distance, that everything was okay, and that we would make it work no matter what. I couldn't tell him I was hurting and that I needed more than what he was giving me. I didn't know what was happening at the time, but now I see it clearly. *I was going through withdrawals.*

I lived each day perpetually suspended between the perception of beauty and the inevitability of chaos; knowing that at any moment, my whole world could come crashing down.

And of course, it did.

Do you know what happens when you take an addict's source away? They find a new one.

Unfortunately for me, I didn't need to look far. I was 22, he was 37, we were both saddened by the perceived neglect from our partners, and decided to seek refuge in one another.

When we first kissed, a terror was born inside my heart. I justified in my mind that I would tell Zed right away, that he would appreciate my honesty and, although it may take time, he would eventually forgive me. He *had* to forgive me.

But I was hooked by this man. A man who was not my love, but loved me so fiercely and so obsessively that I couldn't help but feel powerful. It was easy to idealize someone like him. He devoted himself to whatever I asked of him. "Anything for you my love", he would say. He made it his mission to provide what was missing in my life by adorning me with praise and saying everything my little heart needed to hear to get her fix.

I asked him to learn guitar, desperate to feel the love I had felt before, the joy that came from Jay's purity. I asked him to take me out on adventures, hoping with all my might to feel the expansive playfulness from Zed. But the me who felt alive through the eyes of

HER beloved, SHE was nowhere to be found. After two weeks of this wounded love affair, I was in shambles.

When Zed came to visit, it was inevitable that he would find out. In fact, I think he knew the moment he stepped off that plane, he just didn't want to believe it. When he confronted me, he wouldn't let me near him. I couldn't touch him, hold him, or feel his love. The safe place that was once home, that I had been longing for so desperately since seeing him last, was no longer available.

Not only was I losing him, but I was also losing HER; the vibrant part of me, the part that felt whole, safe, and comfortable in his world. I was terrified that if he were to leave, that SHE would effectively disappear alongside him.

So, I did what most addicts do when backed into a corner, what I had been training to do my whole life. I lied.

IF IT CAN BE DESTROYED BY THE TRUTH, IT DESERVES TO BE

Zed went back to Florida and we decided to work through the feelings of pain, guilt, and betrayal the best we could. We wanted to make it work. In an act of desperation, I was prepared to take this lie to the grave.

The lie to myself: "I've suffered enough to pay tenfold for what happened. Telling him won't do any good."

The lie to him: "In a spontaneous fit of passion, it only happened once."

When bargaining with the part of yourself that knows you are being deceptive, no matter what comes of it, you have already lost.

Low and behold, integrity came knocking at the door that I had bolted, boarded, and barricaded shut. It persisted in the form of a man who, quite literally, barged through my door and threatened to tell Zed the truth if I didn't.

I wish I could tell you that I told him of my own volition, that I stepped up and did 'the right thing' because my desire for truth and integrity was stronger than my fear of what would happen next, but it wasn't. Nevertheless, I told Zed the whole truth, the actual truth, and everything I hated about the truth. This was the intervention I never wanted.

I'll never forget hearing him say the words "You never loved me. If you loved me, you would have never done this to me, or to us." I knew deep down in my heart that I loved this man, and yet I couldn't argue with his logic. Although our relationship did not fully die that day, the pure and innocent parts of it most certainly did, and it was all my own doing.

Realizing your suffering was created by your own choices is a remarkably sobering experience.

DEVOTION

After what can only be described as a total and complete meltdown, I moved back in with my parents, and settled into that all too familiar feeling of utter brokenness.

I couldn't believe I let myself get to this place. It was clear that up until this point there were some very serious flaws in my way of life. Not only was seeking validation and love from others proving to be incredibly unhealthy, but the entire system of relying on external sources to make me feel whole was obviously unsustainable (I am Jack's complete lack of surprise).

Like Bambi trying to find his legs, I timidly began to explore mySELF. An identity of my own had never before concerned me. I realized that outside of what others thought of me, I truly had no idea who I was or who I wanted to be. During the following years I explored, uncovering as many hidden parts of myself as I could and eventually saw an opportunity to cut out the middlemen and go straight to the source, to myself. For the first time in my life, I found *internal* comfort and security.

At the peak of my exploration, I was learning to become a yoga teacher, training as a life coach, working my 9-5 during the week, and at a restaurant on the weekends, and volunteering at a float centre plus two yoga studios, all while learning to run my own business as a virtual assistant. My life was full and it was mine to live—and that excited me.

Within these new tools, I explored the impact of my childhood, the responsibility I felt towards keeping the peace, and the sheer force in which I suppressed my own preferences and desires in order to receive acceptance from others. These painful realizations simultaneously broke me apart while I learned to put myself back together over and over again. Oscillating between experiences of sheer defeat and elated wholeness, I found myself once again face to face with HER.

It wasn't some grand opening to wholeness. There was no epic experience that forever changed my understanding of life, the universe, and everything inside of it. Instead, there were micro adjustments made over a long but devoted period of time. I replaced curating every action I made with learning to create space and search for different choices and finally, I began to make those choices. I was meeting HER and being HER all on my own. It was terrifying at times, and utterly exhilarating at others. *I was beginning to trust myself again.*

Right on cue, and just a little over three years after the day we met, Zed called it. He met another woman and, "Felt something that could be greater than what we had". (You caught that right? The past tense of 'have'!)

My heart all but shattered into a thousand pieces. As much as I knew it was the right thing to do, I did not want to let go. Faced with disaster yet again, I proceeded to use my new tools to break apart the pieces of my life that were no longer working, and put them back together again. This time however, with a little more grace than in the past.

HER

The love I saw and shared in my relationships connected me to the woman I knew I was, and the woman I wanted to become. I got to feel HER grace, beauty, and presence through the reflection in the eyes and heart of my beloved. Yet for all those years, it was not them I yearned to be with so desperately, it was HER.

SHE is a force of nature.

A boundless ocean.

A deep sense of knowing.

And an acceptance of her perpetual broken wholeness.

SHE is integral with herself and can say 'no' with conviction and authority. SHE is resilient, independent, and highly capable of navigating the beautiful chaos of this life. HER chameleon skin is now brilliantly iridescent and instead of being a product of HER wounds, it reflects the wisdom of HER experiences.

In place of my addiction to external validation, I now have the ability to cultivate what I need from within.

If you are ready to call that girl back again, the girl who knows who she is, the one who dances instead of walking, the girl who you know still exists in your heart, it is not too late.

If you feel this same desire for self-sufficiency, then I invite you on this journey of becoming your version of HER.

Of seeing the wholeness in your brokenness.

Of feeling the boundless ocean that exists within you.

Of creating an inner knowing of who you are and what you stand for in this world.

It is because of my experiences, not despite them, that I have learned to support and facilitate this journey within others.

If this chapter has intrigued you... if you feel drawn to learn more about HER, to uncover HER, embody HER, and dance with HER in this life, then I invite you (and HER) to join me.

My dear beloved reader, this lifetime is riddled with challenges big and small.

So again, "I wish you no harm, but may the best disasters come to you." May you be broken by them so you can learn to put yourself back together, stronger than before. May you devote yourself to it so that your growth becomes utterly undeniable.

This is, however, a journey.

There is no arriving.

Only a constant becoming of HER.

ABOUT THE AUTHOR
ANASTASIA VIRGINILLO

Anastasia Virginillo is a Co-Active Coach, Twice Certified Registered Yoga Teacher, Certified Goddess Flow Movement Guide, Tao Healing Hands Practitioner, Master Reiki Practitioner, and Keynote Speaker.

She specializes in serving women who possess a deep desire to build emotional resilience so they can live bravely and with confidence both for themselves, and for those they love. By using tools and strategies grounded in self-development psychology, Anastasia guides you through practical elements of personal development while also integrating principles of energetic mastery.

Anastasia is an adventurer, and a lover of good books, rainy days, and spontaneous dance parties.

Connect with Anastasia
Instagram: @_namastasia

CHEYENNE LINDEMUTH

BRIDGING HELL INTO HEAVEN

INTRODUCTION:

"*I*'ve waded through the river of emotions that come up through the healing process of domestic abuse and narcissistic manipulation. It's not easy. But holding space for your nervous system to relax into what you're feeling and allowing presence for whatever you feel to come up creates a new level of expansion for your nervous system to handle it so it can be released. I know what it feels like to have a broken heart from the one man who was supposed to protect you from it all. I know how bad it hurts when you look in the mirror, and all you see is what they've told you you are; damaged and unworthy. I know what it's like to know how you feel, but not understand why or how to express it. You feel like shattered glass. Like you'll never be able to put the pieces back together. But, the thing is, the beauty in shattered glass is that it gets to be melted down to create something bigger, better, more beautiful and more aligned. Yes, right now, you are shattered glass. But now is your chance to realign yourself with your heart and soul. Become more grounded. Find safety in your emotional body and your inner child. Melt down and recreate yourself from scratch. Remember, love, you're not the result of the cards you were dealt, but a result *of what you chose to do* with the cards you were dealt. Your soul is not broken. Your body is not broken. Your heart is. But my story is proof that your heart can heal.

Cheyenne Lindemuth
Emotional Alignment Coach and Psychic Intuitive

BRIDGING HELL INTO HEAVEN

It's mid-November and today is one of the last 73 degree days we'll have for the season. Windows are wide open and there's a cross-breeze cleansing the energy in my home. I take a deep breath. This moment feels good. It feels aligned.

I am reminded that our relationship with peace is inevitable. These mere passing moments of bliss are already part of our soul's path — in fact, they are glimpses of what our souls will return to once our sacred journey is done. But for now, in this life, that relationship is there, ready to unfold when we're ready to integrate it. The only thing keeping us from experiencing peace is deciding to devote ourselves to the unraveling of anything that has kept us from a constant state of unconditional love.

> *"Nothing real can be threatened.*
> *Nothing unreal exists.*
> *Herein lies the peace of God."*

-A Course In Miracles

I've come a long way to sit here and write these words. I am young, but my life experiences, up to this point, have humbly guided me to understand that the wisdom I have gained — *or more so tuned into* — serves a deeper purpose. My life's journey was not meant to be traveled lightly. And yet, I am here. I've healed, and I'm still healing. I've loved so passionately with everything in my being, and I've laughed so hard I couldn't stand up. I've sobbed hard enough to lose my breath, and I've writhed and seethed at the heartbreaking reality that was my life at one time. Then I turned around and found myself lost in laughter again. There's one truth that has stood the test of time; *someday, you will be okay again.*

Our wounds shape us. So does our truth. How we come into alignment with our truth comes from how we integrate our wounds. The journey of coming home to ourselves is not one that should be riddled with guilt and shame, but with pride and reverence — after all, it is what bridges your hell into heaven.

I remember fantasizing about heaven when I was a child. We lived in an old church that was renovated into a family farmhouse. 16 acres surrounded by pine trees, a vegetable garden, a barn, and a yellow lab — five wonders of a perfect tomboy childhood. I had freedom to run. With my feet in the cool, wet grass and staring in awe at the cotton candy skies, summer nights felt like a dream. I was free. At nightfall, I'd prop my elbows on the sill of my second story bedroom window and stare into the wonderment that was the blanket of stars that twinkled over our huge backyard. *Heaven,* I thought. *This must be what Heaven is like.* A familiar feeling of peace washed over me.

This feeling would later become a checkpoint signal that my body would give me to let me know that everything was going to be okay. I favored night time because cotton candy sunsets let me know that the day was over; the fighting and the abuse would stop for a while. I could rest.

I found peace in Mama Earth. Her grounding comfort felt as safe as the bond I have with my own Mother; who, from day one, until now, is still my very best friend. It was here, in this part of my life, where I learned to seek out nature for comfort. My heaven was my Mama, fresh air, green grass, cotton candy skies, the peepers echoing in the distance, and my lab, Peanut. These things were the perfect embodiment of unconditional love. *These were things I could trust.* My hell was inside that house. Nature would become a foundation to ground me when all else failed.

As an empath and an old soul, feeling the extreme contrast between the soft, nurturing character of Mother Earth, and the cold, devastating suffocation that took place inside those four walls was heavy on my heart. It was enough to make me look to the sky for any sign that there was something more out there. Something I could look forward to that was better. Something that was *whole*.

When the fighting would start, my stomach would turn. The echoes of their yelling would twist my little empath body into knots. My heart couldn't take the level of toxicity that was bubbling over. My father's thundering hollar would vibrate through the floorboards. I'd close my eyes and cover my ears. The cool tears would trace my hot cheeks as I hid behind the couch and prayed for it to stop.

At this point, I was afraid of him, but not in a way that I feared he would come after me. But more so like he was unpredictable. To a degree, I still felt safe. When he was happy, I was happy. When he yelled, I hid. But I knew that it would pass and everything would be okay again. At least until next time.

My Father was the one I looked up to with amazement and wonder. In my sweet, innocent child eyes, he was the coolest guy in the world. At 5' 11", he towered over me — which, at the time, made me feel safely tucked into a big wide world. Sitting on his lap, I could feel his big beefy hands wrapped around me, and I felt like I was on top of the world.

Alongside being an empath and an old soul, I have the unique ability to tune into someone's energy field. I can read what they're feeling, if and how they're suffering, where that stuck energy is located in their energy grids/body, and what traumatic event caused this stuck energy. I find that people have two different reactions when they look me in the eye. Either they love it and want more, or they feel exposed and threatened by my eye contact. With him, it was both. The first, then the latter.

Mama has told me stories about how after I was born, he couldn't take his eyes off me. He loved to hold me and play with me. She tells me stories about his full-belly laughter when I'd endlessly repeat a swear word. She tells me how he couldn't muster up the courage to yell when disciplining me because he thought I was just too precious to hurt. He couldn't help but smile. He loved me. *I was his baby girl.*

Eventually, as I grew out of infancy and aged into my toddler years, I watched the light go out of his eyes for me. Gradually, it changed from love to hatred. Maybe on an energetic level, he felt exposed now that I was older and I could see people on a deeper level. As a daughter who just loved her Daddy so much, who saw him as perfect, and was in complete awe of him, it broke my heart to watch his love for me change. By the time I had turned four, something inside of him flipped like a switch. My half-brother had done something he wasn't supposed to and I got blamed for it. In a fit of rage, he came after me. The sting of his now violent hands against my fragile skin left marks on both my body and my mind. I cried out in pain, absolutely stunned by how quickly and violently he moved. I couldn't sit down for days. This experience shattered the foundation *I thought* I had. One that I would spend the rest of my life recovering from and rebuilding what was broken in an instant. The safety, the trust, the wonderment, and admiration I once had for him was no longer. I couldn't help but feel like something about me was the reason his love turned to hate, but I could never pinpoint a reason to justify his abuse. *There was none.* *"Why, Daddy? How could you hurt me like that?"* I thought. Grief and heartbreak set in. What was once our loving routine of goodnight hugs and kisses had now run cold. The man who was supposed to protect me now became the man I had to protect myself from.

A few years later, Mama and I knew it was time for us to leave. I am forever thankful to have witnessed her unwavering strength and determination in creating our own foundation that was made just for us. One that no one, not even he could destroy. With Mama suffering from a work-related back injury and living on a fixed income, a one bedroom apartment was all we could afford — but it was everything to us. This was the beginning of a new life. *Our* life. The beginning of our *freedom*. This newfound haven would hold us safely for two and a half years until we moved into a bigger apartment in the next town over. Although I now came from a broken home, my heart began to mend.

My father, half-brother, and my lab Peanut all moved in with my grandmother. Mama did everything she could to protect me from the abuse, but because the courts did not want to acknowledge the abuse that was happening, I was still required to do visitation every Wednesday, every other weekend, one week around Easter, and two weeks in July. The mental, emotional, and physical abuse continued. Now, it was more so my half-brother who suffered the physical beatings, but the effects on our young minds were all the same.

Meal times would become a power dynamic of control over us kids. If I didn't finish what was given to me on my plate, I was yelled at. If I *did* finish my plate and asked for more, I wasn't allowed to choose the portion size myself. He chose the portion size, which was always too big for me. When I didn't finish the portions he gave, I was yelled at and forced to stay at the dinner table for up to four hours after dinner to finish what was left. If I still hadn't finished it by then, then I was allowed to put it in the fridge. My punishment was not being allowed to have dessert that evening, or breakfast the next morning. Everyone else got to eat but me. If I got caught trying to sneak a donut or a piece of toast for breakfast, I was screamed at or grabbed. I learned to neglect my body's natural full point and would stuff food down until my plate was empty, no matter how much was on it. I learned how to sneak food up to my room in the middle of the night if I hadn't finished my dinner because I didn't know when my next meal would be. Now I was numb, and disassociating from something that was supposed to nourish me. I was left defenseless; although he was not considered the head of the household, my grandmother still could not brave the idea of standing up to her own son.

The abuse and my now destroyed relationship with food continued through my formative years, and as a result, became second nature to me. As puberty hit, I turned to food for emotional comfort. Emotional eating became my crutch during the abuse as a replacement for his love. It would eventually become a coping mechanism to help me through the bullying I suffered during middle and high school.

Eventually, my half-brother couldn't stand the abuse anymore and got out as soon as he could. He moved to Virginia with his mother. I never got to say goodbye, but when I did get the chance to talk to him on the phone, his voice sounded happier. He was becoming whole again. His senior picture came in the mail and his acne was gone and his smile was sincere. He had found his peace. Although my heart was relieved that he had managed to escape, I was still trying to navigate my hell through and through to no avail.

After each school concert, it was tradition for all the families to meet with their kids in the lobby outside of our auditorium for hugs and pictures. This would be the one and only time that my father would bring me a rose. It was a single red rose wrapped in plastic; and I should have known; the plastic it was wrapped in felt cold. *How eerily similar to the energy in his house*, I thought. I could read in his eyes that there was a reason — not a good reason — for his "loving" gesture. My mom eventually sat me down that following Saturday afternoon and told me the news. It turns out that just hours before my concert that night, my beloved Peanut had passed away. *That rose was a guilt rose*. My ten year old self wailed in her arms as I was stricken with the sudden and unexpected grief. He never had the guts to tell me the truth because he knew her death was his fault. *That was the piece I read in his eyes at the concert that told me something was off*. I had been telling him for weeks to take her to the vet because I could read that her health was failing. He was physically abusing not just us kids, but her, too — he was killing her and I couldn't do a damn thing about it. Again, helplessness and grief set in. I was never told the truth about how she died, nor was I given a chance to say goodbye before she was buried. Another power dynamic for him to control me.

To help me through my grief, Mama helped me pick out a headstone for her. Big promises were made — he would take me to her grave again to place her headstone and I would say my last goodbyes. His empty promises led me on for weeks, and eventually he became angered by my asking over and over. He wouldn't tell Mama where she was buried, and, being so young, I had easily forgotten. Overtime she became a distant memory — the only things I had left of her was a leash, a bowl, a brush, a tennis ball and a few pictures. The pictures and tennis ball I had managed to save and sneak home. The others were a loss.

My grandmother eventually moved in with her fiancé and sold her house. My father decided to buy a house with his girlfriend about forty minutes away. At the time, she was the perfect example of what I considered to be a perfect step-mom. She loved to play games with me and watch sappy rom-coms and make crafts. *Maybe this was someone I could trust.* Despite my high hopes, this trust was broken when she eventually became manic in her emotions towards me. One minute she loved me and the next she couldn't stand me. One day, we were making crafts together and bonding. My trust in her love was growing. Be that as it may, my father pulled in the driveway after work and instantly, her adoration for me changed. "Go to your room so I can *finally* have some peace and quiet for once with your dad!" she snarked. My heart was broken. I ran up to my room and sobbed. *What was it about me that made people change on me like that?* I questioned. Still, I found no answer. Yet again, I was reminded that I could not trust anyone or anything.

As kids, we attach our identities to the things we own. Our dollies, our playhouses, our teddy bears, our puzzles, coloring books, clothes and toys are all things we attach our love to because they provide a sense of attachment and comfort. They make us feel like we have a place. We feel that our toys want us as much as we want them, and our sense of ownership of our toys makes us feel like we are deserving of the play, fun, and joy that will be waiting for us when we're ready. I had moved quite a few of my things from my grandmother's house to Dad's new place, including the cherished things that held memories of my dog Peanut. These were things that I felt would bring me peace and distract me from the whirlwind of emotions I was feeling being around him. During a one week visitation around Easter, the town my dad had moved to was doing a community yard sale. I woke up early one day to find that most of my toys, and even some of my clothes, had been taken out of the room I was sleeping in and were laid out on tables to be sold. In the midst of my freaking out, I begged and pleaded for my things back, but was only met with one impractical demand. "You'll have to *buy* your stuff back if you really want it! You should've thought of that before I put them all out!" he bossed. His words were a perfect example of the narcissistic manipulation I had suffered — *there was no warning*, I recalled. I knew about the yard sale, I knew they were selling a few things, but not *my things*. I *owned them. I shouldn't have to buy them back.* His girlfriend laughed and made a point to call over a mom and daughter walking by to convince them to buy my barbies. Through my raging tears, I watched the little girl walk away happily with my cherished childhood toys. For the hundredth time, my boundaries were crossed. My heart was shattered, and my rage was bubbling up faster than I could handle. I was screamed at and threatened for exploding my furiation, and was expected to stay quiet and deal with it silently.

As time would pass, the weekends I'd spend at his house became all about making sure I didn't make him mad. I walked on eggshells. I was hypervigilant all the time. He started drinking heavier, and thus I became more scared of what might happen. He became abusive in smaller manners, such as demanding that I ask permission to use the bathroom, and him telling me that I was "overreacting" and "didn't *really* have to go" when I got up to use the bathroom. *How could he decide what my body's needs were better than I could?* If I got up during a movie or during the night to use the bathroom, I was screamed at. I became dissociated from my body's natural bathroom cues, and would find myself holding it until I felt like I might burst.

I eventually came to the conclusion that Mama's house, my home, was the only place I could truly feel safe in all aspects.

I was now in the Spring season of my fifth grade year, the last of my elementary years. After months of feeling sick to my stomach every Wednesday and then again every other Friday afternoon knowing that I would have to pack my clothes for a visitation, I decided I'd finally had *enough.* Enough of the heartbreak, enough of the sadness, enough walking on eggshells, and not being able to trust in my surroundings or in him. I was *done.* As we met up at our usual spot that next Friday — *a police station parking lot* — I decided to finally choose *me.* I told Mama what I was going to do. With her encouragement backing me up, I left my suitcase in the back and jumped out of the car, boiling over with about as much confidence and fear that my twelve year old body could hold. "*I've decided* that I will not be going to your house anymore." I stated. Mentally, I gulped. Physically, I stood unyielding in my strength. Angered by my uncompromisable stance, he demanded to speak to Mama. I turned around, got back in the car, and locked the door. Words were spoken between them, and eventually Mama was back in the car and we were back on the road to home. My whole being shook the entire ride. As tears streamed my face, Mama's eyes gleamed with pride in the rearview mirror — she saw her own strength was visible in me. He called me on the phone the following Wednesday afternoon to see if I was coming to spend the evening. I told him one simple word that would set me on my journey to recovery. "*No.*" I said again. *What didn't he understand about what I had said at the station?* My voice shook. My knees felt weak. I felt faint. My heart felt like it was going to beat out of my chest again. Mama stood next to me, tears in her eyes, ready to catch me when I fell, beaming with pride that I stood firm in my decision to choose myself.

"*NO?!*" He exclaimed in a cynical and powerless attempt to gain control back. "...Well... you come here like you're supposed to, or you don't ever come back again. It's all or nothing." he demanded. "*Then I choose nothing.*" I stated with conviction. I felt my power flood my veins. Choosing sovereignty over my health, my recovery, my body's needs, and my emotional needs, meant that I had chosen myself over him again. This would be the one thing he could never take away from me. I felt that same magical heaven-like peace wash over me that I used to feel staring out my bedroom window as a little girl. *Everything really was going to be okay.*

During the early part of the summer after I had finished my fifth grade year, I found out that he and his girlfriend had packed up and took off to — well, I'm not exactly sure where. An array of emotions came over me. I was relieved that I was no longer threatened by his abuse. But my hopeful and naive heart, who ached for her Daddy's love, was grieving the stone cold truth that that was never going to happen. I was heartbroken that he didn't feel I was worth trying to mend his relationship with. After I had told him no, I never wanted to go back in that house; which also meant that I would never get to to take home some of the things that meant the most to me — my only picture of my grandfather that I had who passed away before I was born, and the rest of my very much cherished belongings of my beloved Peanut. Despite all the heartbreak, I knew that this was the beginning of my becoming.

I say "becoming" because I like to see my life's experiences as a chance to become more aligned. Granted, before I could do such a thing, I had to "un-become" everything that I was taught. *This was my chance to bridge my hell into heaven.*

Our bodies are strong. *My* body is strong. She is faithful and able. She is willing and powerful. Unwavering, she carried me through the hardest time of life and gave me the power to stand up to him. So I knew I could trust in her ability to heal. After my nervous system adjusted to the understanding that his presence was no longer a threat, she began to unravel the knot that had been inside of me since I was a child. This was an undoing. Although this truth was a good shock to my nervous system, it was still a shock. My body had never felt this level of safety before. All of those buried emotions came up and my body took the toll. My immune system completely crashed and I was sick for weeks. My scalp became extremely oily and itchy and my nail deteriorated. I lost so much of my hair that I developed a bald spot. I broke out in hives and blisters all over my face, which eventually left a couple minor scars. Mama came through with her knowledge in homeopathic healing and I spent the summer recovering. It's clear that my body was in a deep state of realignment. She was flushing out the toxic energies I had suffered with for such a long time and it was clear — I was being set free.

I spent my middle and high school years navigating the pitfalls of bullies, verbally abusive teachers, puberty and romantic heartbreak. I was the shy one. I kept to myself and observed. I, again, chose the road less traveled and while the rest of my classmates were spending their time earning college credits, I spent mine exploring my soul's artistic expression. I found joy in photography, art, poetry and music — all things that set me free. I found healthy outlets to express everything I'd been through. I decided that my life was for *me* and me only. I realigned my relationship with food and my body. I graduated high school with a 96.4 GPA and headed to a University 680 miles away with Mama by my side. With a heart wide open and a head full of dreams, I set out to change the world. *This was my reclamation.* Deep in my soul was the desire to live a big life — so I made a promise to myself that I would never live two days the same. I set out on a path that would not only aid in continuing the rebuilding of my foundation, but one that would also inspire people to understand that you are not the result of the cards you were dealt, but a result of *what you choose to do* with the cards you were dealt. You don't *have* to look to the future with the expectations of the past, and you are — *and I say this with the deepest love for you and your journey* — always allowed to challenge the narrative you've been given and decide that you want something better. You have the right — *and the power* — to reclaim what it means to live in complete devotion to your becoming. *Me? Well, I've decided to create a new narrative around what it means to be me, fully and completely embodied.*

I am free.
I am, and will always be, the embodiment of love.
I have bridged my hell into heaven.
Like a wolf howling in the distance,
I call back my power.
This is my reclamation.
I am an Emotional Alignment Coach
An artist
A photographer
A poet
A songwriter
A singer
A lover
A dreamer
A trailblazer.
One who will simply not take no for an answer.
As I have awoken the lion inside me,
I am a guide for those who know it's time to do the same.
I hold space for those who are ready to come home to themselves.
This is my prayer for you,
For now and for always.

ABOUT THE AUTHOR
CHEYENNE LINDEMUTH

Cheyenne Lindemuth is an Emotional Alignment Coach and Psychic Intuitive.

Alongside an array of talent in art, photography, poetry, and other mediums, her mission is to guide others through the recognition, release, and realignment of the sacred emotional body and inner child. You can visit her online at www.cheyennelindemuth.com or on instagram at @officialcheyennelindemuth for more details.

Connect with Cheyenne
Instagram: www.instagram.com/officialcheyennelindemuth/
Website: www.cheyennelindemuth.com

DOROTHY KNIGHT

SURRENDER TO THE ALCHEMY OF LIFE

INTRODUCTION:

"*A*re you a Martyr Mama?"

It's easy to become a Martyr Mama. Here's how it evolves.

Once you bring your child into your home and family, you go through the "Fourth Trimester."

Even though you love them beyond measure, you still feel a sense of loss.

Loss for your independence,

Loss for your pre-mom identity,

Loss of your time day-to-day.

This sense of loss is normal for all moms, *but some never get rid of it.*

...Is this you?

I was that mom too.

Motherhood cracked me open.

That's When I Became a 5D Mom.

Now I'm here to guide you on a similar path through spiritual coaching. You'll see your impact expanding beyond your family - and into the world around you. I'm an Embodiment Coach for conscious moms on their journey to an abundance mindset and conscious parenting.

I'm here to help you step into your feminine goddess power.

You CAN have it all

Dorothy Knight
Author and Embodiment Coach

SURRENDER TO THE ALCHEMY OF LIFE

Our human experience often feels squandered by the density of our wounds. We often do whatever we can to suppress and conceal our pain. When the weight of the pain-body is too heavy to carry, God will step in to help us lighten the load. This Divine guidance is often disguised as a "tower moment" when everything comes crumbling down so that we can allow our wounds to be alchemized. Being cracked open, wide open hurts like hell. And it's the only way for the grace of the Holy Spirit to enter. Whenever we say "no" to life, we close the door to our Soul's embodiment. The world needs you open, and God is loving enough to knock more than once. When we open the door and let love in, we surrender to the alchemy of life.

"Mommy, am I safe"? were the words my son whispered when I put a mask on his face for the first time. His big blue eyes looked up at me. I felt a hard lump in my throat as I heard myself say, "Yes, my love. You are safe. Everything is going to be okay." I wasn't sure who I was convincing, myself or him.

I knew what my son's words meant. I felt them in my cells. I remember whispering those exact words to my parents every time they left me with a babysitter while they were working their butts off as immigrants in a new country or flat out left the country for work in my teenage years to support the family. Rejection. Unworthiness. Abandonment. All emotions, deeply rooted in the primal response to fear itself.

Fear took on a whole other level when in March 2020, I, with the rest of this planet, watched as the world changed within the blink of an eye. It all happened so fast. I couldn't believe the whole entire globe would come to a standstill. It didn't make any sense. Emotions bubbled up from the depths of my being that I didn't know existed.

While I watched the wave of dread and fear wash over society, my first reactions were: frustration and anger. And they were completely selfish.

Everyone was home. All day. Every day. My two children and husband. All the time. All their emotions. And all their energy. If you're an empath like me, you know this feeling. It feels suffocating. And if you're an empath, you also know that you're taking on these emotions and energy as your own.

As an energy healer and teacher, I knew I was responsible for my own energy and reality. I thought I had a pretty good handle on it. Everyone always looked to me for comfort, solutions, and solace.

I was well into my spiritual journey since my first awakening back in 2008 when I survived a serious motorcycle accident. While I suffered a concussion and a couple of fractures, it was my Soul that cracked me fully open. God took me away from this Earthly plane for a moment, and while certainly not my first near-death experience, this one literally "knocked some sense into my head."

When I returned to Earth, I received my instructions, and certain codes in my Soul's Blueprint were activated to accelerate my ascension process. I just didn't know it yet, or rather, remember who I really was and what I came here on Earth to do.

At first, all I could feel was anger, frustration, and disappointment. I had been training for months to be in my first triathlon, and not to mention, I had an upcoming trip to go backpacking in Europe the following month.

My ego felt very inconvenienced by this life event.

The concussion opened my crown chakra to receive such high levels of light information, and I had my first glimpses of the fifth dimension and higher. It was overwhelming at times to experience so much energy in my physical body. I felt a different vibration of reality. I saw everyone as energy. I felt everything they felt. It was too much.

I asked God to "dial it down" because I didn't understand, nor was I able to hold so much light and love in my physical body yet. There wasn't enough space in my dense and wounded pain body.

My healing journey was initiated. All levels were calling for understanding, wisdom, and love. My fractures encouraged me to be in bed and recover and rest, something I seldom did in my 3D life. I hated being "still" and alone with my thoughts.

I was an A-type control freak that loved her schedule. Everyone and everything had its place. My gym workout, my career, my friends, my boyfriends, and my vacations all followed in an unconscious pattern.

I was so cruel to my body, putting it to extremes as an obese child, an anorexic teenager, and being a regimented athlete. My body held layers of unresolved trauma, suppressed emotions, and blocked energy. My love-hate relationship with food left me unnourished.

My relationships reflected my fear of intimacy. I was a serial monogamist. I hated being alone, and once in a relationship, no one was allowed to get too close. My friendships were superficial. My career was deeply unfulfilling. I felt the void.

I felt the emptiness inside of me, the longing for something more, something true.

One night as I lay in bed in recovery, I asked God the most important question I was always afraid to ask: "Who am I, and why am I here?"

He responded: "Place your hands upon your injuries every day. You will heal quickly."

I placed my hands upon my injuries. I immediately felt the warmth and healing light emanate from the palm of my hands. I didn't even know what Reiki was at the time. Night after night, I tended to my wounds.

Day after day, the doctors and physiotherapists marveled at my "speedy recovery" attesting it to my youth and good health. Their hypothesized prognosis for my recovery of several months went out the window, and within a month, I was backpacking through the Alps.

It was my first conscious experience of collapsing time. And it felt so liberating!

As I continued raising my body level awareness, I knew I could heal my PCOS, chronic headaches, and premature arthritis.

I began to marvel at my miraculous body and understood that it was my greatest compass. My body was always "talking to me." I just didn't listen.

I completely shifted my relationship with my body and knew my rigorous training wasn't in alignment with my wellbeing. I attended my first yoga class and immediately fell in love with the simplicity and deep invitation of the practice to weave movement with the breath.

I discovered what chakras were and deepened my understanding of the body's energy centers and systems. I went into total information and learning mode. Whatever spiritual books I could get my hands on, I absorbed all the information instantly.

Within a year, my PCOS was gone. My headaches subsided, and the arthritis in my knees dissolved.

They say, "time heals." I say, "time reveals." And we will repeat what we don't repair.

As time went on, I brought beautiful balance back into my body. I had a regular yoga practice and made time for self-care and nourishment. So, God decided I was ready for my next initiation: unconditional love.

In 2010, I was in the most toxic relationship of my life. No one understood how I could put up with such an asshole that put me and everyone around him down. He was also a narcissist. And I attracted this perfect narcissistic mirror into my life.

He, of course, wasn't like that when I first met him. He was tall, dark, and handsome. He was athletic, well-traveled, and educated. He appeased my ego very well. The relationship moved very quickly, and we bought a house together.

That was when Dr. Jekyll introduced Mr. Hyde.

He was manipulative, verbally abusive, and self-centered. He constantly compared me to his perfect mother, was solely focused on his own pleasure, and picked at every flaw he could find in me. Maybe it was the Virgo in him, but I thought, "deep down, there's a good person in there. I can save him."

I spent months putting up with his tyranny. I started to hate that house and being in it. I would hide at work, take any overtime I could, plan my workouts and outings for when he would be home— anything not to be there.

I never looked more forward to Mondays in my life.

During this time, I was working as a Government Clerk, basically a paper pusher. While the job was just about as fun as watching paint dry on a wall—actually, watching paint dry was more fun, I did it once when the office was repainted—the one thing that made it fun was my colleagues.

There were a handful of us "misaligned misfits" that only needed that paycheck until something better came along. It's amazing how you'll meet Soul Family in the most interesting of places.

There was one Soul contract that was activated within this group. He was also tall, dark, and handsome. His sparkly green eyes soothed me in the best of ways. I felt their gaze into the depths of my soul on a level I had never experienced before. He made me laugh, he saw my potential, and he became my saving grace.

There was undeniable chemistry between us which I know we were both terrible at hiding. We at least tried to play it cool because we were both in other relationships. Energy knows energy, and the alchemy ignited.

Our souls danced happily together in secret. He was unhappy with his relationship, and I was unhappy with mine. My heart already decided that I would leave my relationship to be with him, like literally, in a heartbeat. And yet, he couldn't do the same. He felt he couldn't leave his partner because of his responsibilities to her and her family.

I was so certain this was my soul mate, and we could be happy together. I thought he would inevitably come to the same conclusion and leave that relationship. He showed me what was possible in love, and there was no way I was going to let that go.

Back at home, I knew it was only a matter of time, and I would be free of the toxicity permeating through the walls into my now separate bedroom. As his anger grew, I was afraid to fall asleep. I was so desperate to shut off my mind and rest, I opened the bedside table drawer and found the painkillers the doctors prescribed to me after my motorcycle accident.

I looked at the pill bottle, intact and sealed, and convinced myself, "just this one time."

That one time became many times.

Now who was the real Dr. Jekyll and Mr. Hyde?

I was happy-go-lucky at work and miserable and depleted at home.

One night, even the painkillers couldn't soothe me to sleep. I felt the torment of my troubled soul and said, "God, why do I feel so alone?! I don't want to be here anymore!"

God replied: "Then leave."

It was so simple. So obvious. How did I not come to that conclusion on my own?

The following day when he left for work, I packed whatever belongings I could and left everything behind. I moved back with my parents, which as a then 29-year-old, felt like an epic failure. But I knew it would be better than what I was leaving behind.

Despite the supposed setback in life, I felt a glimmer of hope. I told my beloved soulmate what had happened, thinking it would nudge him in the same direction to make that leap.

He didn't. In fact, he did a complete 180' on me. When I saw the look in his eyes, I felt my heart drop into my stomach as he uttered, "I can't be with you." Rejection. Unworthiness. Abandonment. I felt all my inner child wounds flare up like fireworks.

I couldn't be with him; I couldn't be around him. I couldn't be in that office anymore. My wounded ego activated a familiar program of self-sabotage. I knew my job contract was up for renewal, and I did everything I could to be let go.

My plan worked. I took my remaining vacation time out and booked myself a trip to the Bahamas, solo. It was my first time traveling alone. As soon as I arrived, many propositions came my way as men assumed I came single and ready to mingle. All I wanted was to be alone and lick my still very raw wounds. I wasn't in the mood for rebound sex. Instead, I gifted myself with a journal, and for the first time in years, I let it out on paper. I wrote. I cried. I wrote some more. I wrote until I had nothing left in me. Just as I was about to close the journal and crawl into bed, my eyes gravitated to the last page of writing. I found myself reading the words aloud. I felt the energy. I felt the pain. I felt the power they held over me.

I closed the book and sat on the floor in front of the full-length mirror in my hotel room. I gazed deep into my eyes. I sat there for a long time, watching the energy shift in my gaze each time a thought, an emotion, or a memory passed. Then a calmness swept over me. I sat with everything. I sat with nothingness. I asked this inquisitive reflection, "who are you?"

I saw a flicker in her eyes, a smile in the corners of her mouth, and a surge of energy rise from within me as I screamed at the top of my lungs like a wolf crying beneath a full moon.

Her fire had awoken me and made me feel something I remembered long ago. I stood up and went back to my journal. For the first time, I wrote down everything my heart truly desired in a relationship and in life. Also, for the first time in my life, I surrendered myself to the unknown and decided to trust the divine timing of God.

I met my husband a week later. I met my husband a couple of times prior to this. Soulmates travel in the most divine of ways. As a child, I lived on the same street as my husband but didn't know him directly. We played amongst each other with common friends already activating our soul contract for a future timeline.

I met my husband a year before leaving that toxic relationship. I was with my ex at the movies, and we bumped into him and my husband's ex. Our eyes connected, and it was complete soul recognition. This connection felt so familiar and significant. It was only a few seconds that our eyes met, but it felt like a wonderful eternity of bliss.

As we parted ways, I asked my ex: "Who is that? He replied: "That guy lived in my house before my family bought it."

My husband lived in the exact same house that my ex lived in, in his exact bedroom on the exact same street that we both grew up in.

If that wasn't a sign of alignment and synchronicity, heaven help me! Yet, at the time, I didn't really think much about it. My soul had to complete the previous contract first.

I returned from my Bahamas trip in full-blown golden goddess mode and decided to throw myself an epic birthday party. One friend offered to drive me and said he was bringing a friend along. When I got into the car, my eyes locked in with the beautiful soul from a year prior. My husband said, "you look familiar—have we met before?"

We were inseparable that night. We danced, we laughed, we talked, and our beautiful relationship unfolded. He treated me like a queen. He was so open, honest, kind, and loving—it was too good to be true. A relationship couldn't possibly be this "easy." A familiar script started penetrating my mind. I was waiting, almost expecting the relationship to hit some sort of tower moment when everything would come toppling down, just like the ones before him. I put my guard back up. I didn't trust him. What was he hiding? My madness consumed me so much, and I decided to break up with him.

I heard the unconvincing words come out of my month on that breakup phone call. I knew I couldn't do it in person because my soul didn't believe me. I hung up. It was done. I was all alone again. Rejected. Unworthy. Abandoned. This time of my own doing.

My husband wouldn't have it, though. Like a knight in shining armour, he arrived and said he didn't believe me. He just knew we weren't meant to be together, and he wasn't going anywhere.

I stared at him in disbelief. No one had ever fought for me before. No one had shown me so much love. He saw beyond any façade I could put on and disabled every defense mechanism I could throw his way. He was the divine masculine in ways I had never experienced before. My heart was completely cracked open to fully receiving his love.

We got married a year later, and I was pregnant with my first child a month after. God presented me with my next initiation: Sacred Divine Embodiment.

Motherhood can feel like joy and grief simultaneously. All of us go through the "fourth trimester" You see this beautiful child birthed through you, you love them beyond measure, and at the same time, you consciously or subconsciously experience a sense of loss. This experience is a redefining moment for many moms, and some make it a permanent thing and continue with life as "martyr mama." I was that mom.

I consciously decided to be a stay at home for both of my children. I wanted to be there for them where I felt short changed as a child. I never wanted them to feel rejected, unworthy, or abandoned. I adjusted my entire life to be in sync with my children. Their needs always came first.

I knew these children were superconscious little beings with big energy and even bigger love. I knew that they chose me to be their mother. And I knew I would do everything in my power to ensure their health and wellbeing. Despite its challenges, I truly enjoyed the early years of motherhood, where life seemed so simple.

When both of my children reached school age, I felt a familiar void inside. My days felt different, having more time on my hands. I accepted that it was time to do more things with my life and made my debut back into the working world as a yoga teacher. I got a part-time gig at a local gym and quickly found my calling as an energy teacher.

It felt incredible to create such a positive impact for other people every day. I could feel how people would drag the weight of the world onto the yoga mat and transmute the energy to feel lighter and brighter. I was in my flow and became a Master Manifestor. I decided to override the 9-5 paradigm and set forth to manifest a new reality.

In 2019, I launched my business—my reiki practice. Becoming an entrepreneur and birthing my business was one of the most terrifying, exciting, and challenging things I've ever done, and it has changed my life completely. I stepped into my soul's calling and found a way to use my energy to serve others and create win-win-win situations. I discovered that work-life alignment is possible. I thought I had "arrived" until "Mommy, am I safe"? were the words my son whispered when I put a mask on his face for the first time.

Rejected. Unworthy. Abandoned. Society rejected my stance on this world event, and I was now deemed unworthy to be amongst the public. Many friends, colleagues, and family vibrated out of my life because I didn't sway in my truth.

The world is permeated with chaos and confusion.

Every morning, I woke up to chaos. My husband was trying to work while my daughter and son were running amok behind him. It was me chasing my children to get them settled for another long day of online learning while forgetting to eat my breakfast to make sure they were understanding what was being taught and trying to catch up with the pile of dishes in the sink, figuring out how to survive through another day.

While there were certainly bigger things to be concerned with in the world, the world inside my home was becoming more concerning, and the once perfectly organized me felt anything but organized. I felt like I was taking care of three, and there was nothing left for me.

I would crawl into bed at the end of each day, my husband reaching over to caress me, and I would find myself pulling away, not wanting to be touched, let alone "put out" for him. I put myself out all day for everyone. I wanted space. I wanted silence. I wanted to just "be."

I homeschooled the kids during the day and worked on my business at night. I was exhausted and frustrated. And now my kids were starting to feel it. My husband was feeling it. And my clients were feeling it.

I didn't know what more I could do or offer to change the situation. I had total mom guilt with my kids. I felt so disconnected from my husband. My house felt perpetually messy. I lived in yoga pants yet never had time to do yoga anymore. What happened to ME?

One night, while trying to meditate, I felt the pain surface as I looked up at the ceiling and heard myself sob, "God, I cannot carry all of this anymore! Why am I so alone and unsupported?"

In the depths of my despair, God responded, "You're never alone, and you never asked."

Those words left me sitting in silence for a long time.

They were completely true.

If the world felt "broken" it was because I felt "broken" within. I knew my outer world was only a reflection of my inner world. Heaven and hell both exist on Earth, and it was entirely up to me to decide which reality I created.

No one rejected me. No one deemed me unworthy. No one abandoned me. That was all me.

I rejected me. I believed I was unworthy. I abandoned myself.

I needed all of me for this human experience and the truth: I was already whole.

That night I was cracked open, and God's love poured into me, cleansing me, releasing me from my ego, my wounded child, my unexpressed soul. My divine feminine and divine masculine aspects weaved their way into one another, and my Soul mission was on.

In the last six months, I have made two massive timeline jumps. The first was moving away from the city into nature which was the perfect container for my husband and me to rise and vibrate higher. I loved living embraced by nature, connecting with Earth, and serving from such grounded energy.

I felt being in this place was a quantum leap into the timeline my heart truly aligned with and desired. I had been dreaming about living in a tropical place for over a decade. I just couldn't wrap my head around the "how" part.

I didn't resonate with the reality that was being given to me, so I knew that the universe was supporting me to finally go for it and jump right on into Costa Rica.

And for the first time, my husband felt it was possible too. We set our intention, and the next six months prepared us for our piece of paradise.

It was divine alchemy in motion. As a partnership, we built the momentum to anchor in our timeline. Not to say that it didn't come without challenges. There was so much resistance coming our way from others and situations it was tempting to question if this move was truly a possibility. But we stayed in our lane, homed in our manifestation vibration no matter what anyone thought, said, or did.

Whenever we're about to make a massive shift in life, resistance will always come. It's the universe checking to see how badly we really want what we're asking for.

It's surreal typing these words, feeling the sun on my face, a warm breeze caressing my skin, and a lush jungle surrounding me. I am in my "Pura Vida." My journey has cracked me open more than once to finally living a life of abundance in alignment with who I really am.

I want you to live a life of abundance in alignment with who you really are. To discover your true self, what you want, and how to receive it.

I'm here to help you shift that paradigm and uncover those roots to discover your most empowered self and shift from "martyr mom" to "5D mom." Let's unearth your passions, find your alignment, and take that leap to manifest your paradise.

Our 1:1 Coaching Opens a Portal. From overwhelmed, burned-out mom in crises to powerful creatress of your relationship, your family, and your abundant life.

You'll get your power back. You'll redirect and overcome the stories you've been telling yourself. You'll ignite consciousness, intimacy, and truth within yourself and your family. Are you ready to dive into what's holding you back and open the portal to your most empowered self?

ABOUT THE AUTHOR

DOROTHY KNIGHT

Dorothy Knight is an Author and Embodiment Coach. Her coaching programs have helped hundreds of clients heal unresolved trauma and embody their full potential. She is passionate about empowering her clients towards self-mastery, illuminating the way to fulfilling their soul mission with passion, purpose, and play.

Before becoming an entrepreneur, Dorothy got her degree in Journalism New Media from Sheridan College Institute of Technology and Advanced Learning. After that, her path shifted into holistic health, and she received her teacher training in yoga. Dorothy is also a certified Reiki Master, Ohana Generational Healer, and Conscious Parent Educator. As an author and Soulpreneur, she travels and teaches in some of the most beautiful places on Earth. Dorothy is still a "stay-at-home mom," homeschooling her two children while running a successful 7-figure business and writing books.

She currently lives in Costa Rica with her husband and two children.

Connect with Dorothy
Website: 5dmom.com
dorothyknightreiki.ca
Instagram: @5dmom
Facebook: @the5dmom
LinkedIn: www.linkedin.com/in/dorothy-knight-b339253a/
Twitter: https://twitter.com/the5dmom
YouTube: www.youtube.com/channel/UCAKz7CNjzqtItgoMhG9Ko-
A?view_as=public

DR. FALAK SHAIKH

RISE TO YOUR SOUL'S CALLING

INTRODUCTION:

*A*re you a Healer's Soul, yet you fear putting out yourself as one and are too afraid to be seen and heard?

Are you playing small and hiding, because of this unusual fear of being misunderstood, or rejected by people, or even extreme fear of being persecuted?

Are you dimming away your light by offering your services for free or charging very little, as you were told healing should be for free?

If you feel it's only you feeling this way, then let me tell you "You are not alone." I have been there and I exactly know how you are feeling.

What if I told you that you don't have to do that anymore.

It is possible to put out yourself, to outshine and embody your healer self without fear and live a life soulfully aligned to your purpose of making a living out of it.

With my journey of Healing the Healer within me and helping several clients do the same, I can also help you heal the "wounded Healer" within you.

My purpose on this earth is to heal and serve those who can heal and serve several others.

Are you ready to heal the healer within and live a life aligned with your soul's purpose?

Be ready to be seen, put yourself out, and outshine in the world as a healer. Embody your healer self and live your life's purpose of healing and service. Use your unique gifts, talents and live your soul's calling without fear or doubt. Know your worth and value of your energy that you are investing and have people who reciprocate for the same by paying you what you deserve. Believing in oneself without feeling like an imposter. Take responsibility for healing the self first as that is going to help heal others more effectively and powerfully.

Carl Jung the founder of Analytical Psychology emerged as a healer whose skills arose from having first attended to the wounds in his own soul.

It's high time hiding and playing small, it's time to shine the light of your soul and do what you were meant to do, ie. healing.

Let me tell you, if you are not showing your light to the world, you are not only doing a disservice to yourself but also to all those people who you are meant to serve, who are waiting to be healed and transformed through you. So stop waiting at the shore, dive deep into the ocean to discover the pearl of the sacred purpose of living your Soul's Calling.

Dr. Falak Shaikh
Intuitive Energy Healer, Relationship Coach, Best Selling Author, and Homoeopath

RISE TO YOUR SOUL'S CALLING

Being a lightworker or a healer, one often feels the sole responsibility is to help others heal. And in this, one might miss the most important person, and that is yourself. As a healer, it is our first responsibility to heal the "SELF". You can only help others heal and go deeper into oneself as much as you have for yourself.

And when we women, healers, lightworkers, and torch-bearers are unhealed and wounded, we hide, dim our light, and fail to rise in our full potential and power.

The world needs you, me, and so many of us. If you keep hiding and dimming your light, you are not only doing a disservice to yourself but also others as they are waiting to be healed and transformed by you.

One can only imagine if all healers take responsibility for healing themselves first, then how much healing and transformation we can bring on this earth. Not only that, by rising in our true self as healers, shining and putting out ourselves in the world, we can flourish and have abundance by living our soul's purpose.

I am here to share my story of healing and transformation as a woman, as a healer, as someone who has aligned her work with her soul's calling and purpose, to help you introspect and ignite your journey of healing the healer within, own your unique gifts and talent and flourish bringing in alignment with your soul's purpose. Through this, you would be able to recognize all those parts of you that you had been avoiding looking at and that are blocking you from being seen and flourishing.

It was November of 2018, a chilly morning in Toronto. I was walking my son to school with my daughter in the stroller, and it was pouring rain. By the time we reached school, my son was almost wet, my daughter was crying as she was cold, and in spite of us wearing our jackets, we were wet and cold. We were new to the city and unprepared for these rainy winter days. Heading back home with my wet boots and my coat drenched, I hated this land to the core. That day when I went home, I regretted moving to Canada. I had no driver's license yet, so I couldn't drive. I was a stay-at-home mom and dependent on my husband for everything—from being a well-established Doctor with a practice of over 15 years and having a well-established clinic and assistant professor in a medical college. I felt from Dr. Falak Shaikh, I was nobody, since I could not use my Doctor credential here and nobody knew me. I left not only my family and friends back in India, but I felt as if I left my whole identity behind. I felt as if this new country had taken away my identity. I was no longer a doctor here—I was a homoeopathic practitioner here. And I could only practice after getting registered, which might take months. I could see my eight and half years of education in the medical field going down the drain. It was a huge blow to my Ego. An ego that was built over the years that defined me for who I was. I felt as if I was nothing. What do I address myself as? Who am I? I am Nobody. Nobody knew me in this new land, and I have no friends, no family, and no sense of identity. My heart wept, and there were days I would cry and feel hopelessness and despair. I don't know what was more painful, the pain of leaving the family and friends and the known or losing my identity and the blow on my Ego. I was depressed for days, and then I moved into a state of desperation. Desperation to find my new identity and start working which would make me feel worthy, that I am something, and without it, I felt like "Nothing". Every day I would look for some or other training or certification that I could do, and my dear husband would calmly listen and also help me with his analytical mind of all the pros and cons of doing it.

I was already a certified yoga teacher also with other healing modalities like Reiki, Theta Healing, EFT, Ancestral Healing, Sixth Sense Healing, Crystal Healing, and so many other healing modalities. But still, I felt I needed more certifications, degrees to prove that I was worthy, to the point that I was ready to go to college again, get a degree in Naturopathy and be a doctor again.

I was so attached to the 'Dr.' title that I failed to see myself beyond that.

I felt I was thrown off my centre, and I was so confused, clouded, and desperate.

I did not know what path I wanted to walk. And let me tell you, for anyone else except me, it would be just a phase of transition, but for me, it was like living a nightmare. As if my biggest fear had manifested. My greatest fear of becoming like my mother— dependent, helpless, and weak.

My mother was a homemaker, a woman who was not much educated as her father did not want her to, as having a daughter was a liability for him and got her married to a man of his choice. When I was a kid, I have a very clear memory of my mom running out of the house as my father tried to hit her. This scared the shit out of me. As a six-year-old, I felt so helpless. I could only think how I could save her from him, and naturally, I looked at my father as a villain of our lives. When I grew up as a teenager and saw the dysfunctional relationship between my parents, I asked her why she didn't leave him if she wasn't happy? And she said, "If only I was educated enough and was financially independent, I would have walked out," and hence I had one mission in life, to be INDEPENDENT in every way so that I don't have to be dependent on anyone in my life. And this situation was exactly making me feel what I feared the most, fear of ending up like my mother. Though my situation was not even close to what she had experienced in her life, I had a super supportive, loving husband who was even ready to support me if I wanted to go to college again. But it is the stories that we tell ourselves in our head, the fears we have in our hearts, and a reality we see that never existed.

Only when I let go of the fear and healed this pattern in me could I let go of the desperation to make money and be independent. I realized in desperation to be independent and make money, I had missed seeing the beauty of the new land, did not allow myself to enjoy life itself and my vision had become linear.

This healing and awareness helped me to be at peace being a homemaker and having an opportunity to be available to my three-year-old daughter, and five-year-old son felt like a blessing. I took off the glasses that saw a homemaker as being unworthy, passed on by my mother, and the fear of being suppressed as a woman if I am being dependent on my husband. I healed the wounded feminine in me to be able to lean back in my feminine essence and opened up to receiving instead of doing everything all by myself, like making my own money. I realized this new land was making me heal my wounded feminine and wanted me to move into BEING rather than DOING.

I began to start settling into the new land, started making some new friends, and simply enjoyed life as it flowed. However, now my exploration of various options for my work did not come out of a place of desperation. I saw the blessing in disguise that I had the liberty to take time to soul search what is that my soul wants to express through me, what does it want to do.

I had realized by now, the only way out is to go within. It was at a point to decide whether to begin my new journey, get a degree again in Naturopathy or pursue a career with all the skills and certifications I had in my bucket. Meanwhile, I participated in an Ayahuasca Ceremony where I experienced my soul for the first time ever in my life. It was so beautiful with tears of bliss that flowed and with the message, "The soul is so magnificent that it doesn't need any certification to shine. You just need to allow your light to shine through you."

And that was the point I decided to drop the idea of doing any courses or certifications.

The only thing I could see myself was a healer, this is what I was in my soul. I had been a doctor of Homoeopathy, which is a holistic way of healing, and I integrated other energy healing modalities for my patients and clients to help them heal. I was yet to get registered as a Homoeopath as it was still in process, and meanwhile, what I could put myself out as and practice was only as an Energy Healer.

I had always addressed myself as a doctor. I had never talked about the energy healing modalities that I practiced. Only if anyone would ask me or be interested would I talk about it and disclose that "yes, I am an energy healer as well." I remember there was a person who looked at me with suspicion when she entered my clinic and saw crystals around. Once a patient walked into the clinic unannounced and saw me giving a healing session to a person with crystals laid all over her body, and she was convinced I was a witch who takes people under her control—haha. I didn't want to scare people away by exactly telling them what I do, as that was beyond the understanding of their limited logical, linear mind. I remember when I first took my mother for a reiki healing session, and the healer was cleaning her aura she got so scared and left the session in the middle, she didn't get what was actually happening.

When I realized that this is what I am, a Healer, all my fears started crawling out from their ambush. Meanwhile, in India, a fanatic political leader was about to win an election and viewing it all over the news enraged me. I didn't want him to come to power, imagine not even living in India was so affected by it.

One day when I was sharing it with my husband, he asked me what about him is affecting you so much? And as I also knew, the world is just a mirror of who you are, and whatever is triggering you is mirroring certain aspects of you.

It was a memory that triggered it. In 2002, in India, under the leadership of this political leader, there were riots in the name of religion, and I saw mobs of people with weapons in their hands raving to kill the minority. My family belongs to the minority, and they were scared for their lives. This triggered the fear in me that if he came into power again, I would be persecuted and killed. It was basically the fear of being attacked, killed, and persecuted that had surfaced through this incident.

When I sat with this feeling and meditated with it, with a healer who held space for me to go within, a vision flashed in front of me, and I saw myself being tied to a pole and a bunch of people in front of me ready to burn me—I could see myself being burnt alive. It was because I couldn't explain to them what I was doing. I was a healer, and people couldn't understand what I was doing, and that scared them, they tagged me as a witch, and I was gone.

I had locked that memory in me. Then I was shown the whole purpose of me being a doctor in this lifetime, and having studied science, I had bridged the gap that I had experienced in the previous lifetime, and here I was to learn myself to embrace my healer self and bridge it up with science so that I can take healing to even the logical, linear minds.

This was me embracing my healer self. I also dropped my Dr title from my social media profiles, and I was ready to shine the light of the soul.

I started putting myself out there as a healer, and that is where I began my journey of being an Intuitive Energy Healer, spiritual entrepreneur, and writing my first book, The Soulmate Mantra, which is now a bestseller.

In February 2020, I went back to India to visit my family, and then the life-changing event of all of humanity happened, the lockdown. My husband had left for Canada, and my kids and I got stranded in India. I had to stay in India for months till flights opened up.

Lockdown has been life-changing for many of them, and I was no different.

I had to stay with my mother, and guess what? All my mother's wounds surfaced. As I came face to face with all my wounding and patterns with her and healed, just the next day, I started channeling Archangel Metatron, Goddess mother Isis, and Light Language.

It was as if my spiritual journey was on fire. Every night I would have channeled messages and downloads with Light Language transmission and light code art.

I was asked to share it with people and spread the transmission to as many people as possible. However, with the witch's wound, I was scared to share it online, feeling people wouldn't understand and would be questioned, so I kept it hidden and was playing small, not putting it out, only sharing it with people who knew about it. Again, I was given a message to spread. And then, one day, I was asked by a woman who has her YouTube channel to interview for her channel and share all about light language. I was super nervous, and hence I asked all the guides, masters, and source/creator to assist me. When I asked, "What would I say? What is light language, and how does it work?" I was shown the whole scientific explanation of working of the light language with the theories of quantum physics. My mind was blown away, and now I could explain and talk about light language to anyone and explain it to all the logical minds. I was shown that science and spirituality are not different. Energy healing is no woo woo. And it can be understood even by a lay person who has no background in energy healing. I had fully embraced and integrated the healer within, and I was no longer afraid of putting myself out as a healer and talking about all that I do. I did the interview with ease and grace, and then onwards, I have not stopped putting myself out and owning myself fully and completely.

If someone doesn't believe in past lives or does not recall one, I want to tell them that what their ancestors have experienced is passed over to them through the lineage and is shared over through time and spaces by the mass consciousness. Therefore they might not be the one who was persecuted, but still, the experience gets locked in the subconscious or the unconscious. Often wanting to hide and playing small is an unconscious response to the generational pattern that is being locked in.

Science has actually been able to demonstrate generational wounding on the level of DNA. In a 2013 article published by Dan Hurley in Discovery Magazine, entitled, Grandma's Experiences Leave a Mark on Your Genes, it stated:

According to the new insights of behavioral epigenetics, traumatic experiences in our past or in our recent ancestors' past leave molecular scars adhering to our DNA. Jews whose great-grandparents were chased from their Russian shtetls; Chinese whose grandparents lived through the ravages of the Cultural Revolution; young immigrants from Africa whose parents survived massacres; adults of every ethnicity who grew up with alcoholic or abusive parents; all carry with them more than just memories.

The witch hunt was real. It is estimated that in the witch-hunts and trials of our human history, over 13 million women were killed in gruesome, torturous ways in Europe and North America alone from the 14th century to the 17th century. This is not even taking into account other cultures that have vilified women, their intuition, and their relationship with healing and nature and persecuted these women for being evil, of the devil, or possessed in some way. All of this was done in the name of patriarchal authority, to devalue and rob women of their power and their roles of influence in society.

The first crime for which women were persecuted was for possessing any healing abilities, be it energy healing or knowledge of herbs or medicines from nature. Such medicine women and healers were considered to have made a pact with the devil by the religious heads. And I have experienced those sarcastic comments for me as well, of being a witch who practices black magic. But they failed to understand the power and wisdom of these medicine women because they are in tune with nature, with the earth, and with the spirit/divine/source/creator.

The history of witches is, after all, a history of the persecution of women, or as author and theorist Eric Jong called it, a gendercide.

Does that sound familiar? India, the land where I was born and raised—I should be happy that I survived being a girl child. Not many women get that opportunity to be born when they are killed in their wombs for being a woman. And it's not centuries ago that I am talking about, but it's what I have seen when I was growing up. Then, a law was passed, and disclosing the gender of the child to the parents is now considered a crime in India to protect the girl child as it had gone too far due to the imbalance between the ratio of between men and women. In fact, when I grew up, one of my aunts told me how upset my mother was on finding out that I was a girl, as girls are considered to be a liability and boys as a resource. However, it took me a while to heal the wound and trauma around being born as a woman. And here I am, embracing every inch of being a woman. Do you realize your power girl? This patriarchal society is so scared of you for even being born, and you are busy hiding your gifts and power.

I have worked with so many women who were rejected for being a girl by their caregivers, parents, or relatives and are so scared to own their feminine energy. Rather, they cut off from their femininity and adapt to the masculine way of being. They feel highly uncomfortable being a woman, dressing up or adorning things that make them feel like a woman, getting attention in any way. As they feel unsafe being a woman. So, what do they do? Hide and play safe. Do not show up.

Yet, the second crime that women were persecuted for was gathering of any kind, specifically gathering without men or holy men from the churches.

A book released at the end of 1400 by Heinrich Kramer, "The Hammer of the Witches" stated that "The woman who thinks alone, thinks evil." Are you aware that still in places like Saudi Arabia, Afghanistan, and maybe so many other monarchist countries, it's a crime for women to go out alone or without a man. So what has happened in ancient history has not yet been completely eradicated from the world, it still prevails, and this is shared in the consciousness of women through collective consciousness.

There was a behavioral study of a troop of Japanese monkeys on the island of Kōjima. The scientists observed that some of the monkeys learned to wash sweet potatoes that they were given to eat. Gradually, this new potato-washing habit spread through the troop—in the usual fashion, through observation and repetition. And this spread instantly spread across the water to monkeys on nearby islands.

I am not surprised how a wound around women is passed from generations after generations across lands and seas and still finds life in their unconscious and subconscious.

Just a year ago, I had a calling to start an online sisterhood circle, with an intention to hold space for women to help them rise in their divine feminine essence and build a community of women who support each other and fix each other's crown. Out of all the women who joined the group, only a few would show up as they met one gathering after another. I had to put a question in the group and ask what was stopping them from showing up for the gathering. And guess what? Most women messaged me personally that they felt uncomfortable and they were struggling to break their shells. I could see the same wound playing out in women who are struggling to show up in groups with other women. I feel honoured that I am able to hold space for women and gently hold them as they break out of the cocoon and are ready to be transformed.

Yet, another crime for which women were persecuted was for sexual expression. In so many cultures and traditions, the sexuality of women is considered to be evil, where they have the power to enchant men and take them away from spirituality. It is women who are responsible for misleading men and were considered to be possessing evil powers, where men had no power but to give in. Does that sound familiar? Have you heard society still accusing women and holding them responsible for their abuse or sexual assault by blaming them for exposing their skin or the way they are dressed? Do you know why women are asked to be covered so that men aren't provoked? I was born in a traditional Muslim family and had a conservative father. He was the police in the house who kept a check on how I dressed, and showing skin was an absolute no-no. It took me years of healing to be comfortable in my own skin as I was shamed so much for my body and what I wore. After all, he has his own wounded masculine who was controlling and oppressive. And I had my lesson of standing up for what I believed in. A perfect match, soulmates, isn't it? (I am glad I could heal my wounds around my father and could convey that I loved him before he passed away.) In so many ways, the expression of women has been shut off by the patriarchy, and it's so subtle that it's almost considered a normal way of being. This is the patriarchal wounding that has put women and their sexuality into a box. If she expresses her sexuality, she is a whore or a slut. Did you know many parts of the world, female circumcision still prevails in the name of religion?

This sexual energy is the creative energy, and when it is not flowing, expressed, or suppressed, one tends to shut off the creative gifts that they are born with. All those gifts that are waiting to birth through you into the world so that you leave your own unique imprint in the world, living your soul's calling and purpose.

So how do these wounds play out?

• Fear of using your gifts and adapting to the more acceptable credential, as I had been doing most of my life.

• Wanting to hide and not be seen or heard.

• Fear to put out oneself on social media, online, or even talk about oneself as that would bring in too much attention to you.

• Not standing up for oneself.

• Fear of Disapproval, hence seeking approval and pleasing others.

• Squeezing oneself in by trying to fit in, to avoid standing out and taking space.

• Afraid to put out creativity in the world, be it through healing, art, dance, using voice in the form of singing or playing small so as to avoid the limelight through their gifts, choosing to stay small and avoid rising in their power.

• Shutting off the intuition and intuitive gifts, or afraid of it.

• Feeling that one is too much to handle, feeling judged/ostracized, and a deep fear of being hurt or killed for being you and fully opening up to your gifts, or so-called weirdness, etc.

• Fear of owning your power or misusing it, hence lacking trust and belief in oneself.

• Feeling ashamed for one's sexual expression or sexuality.

• Feeling disconnected from one's feminine essence or sexuality often leading to infertility, absence of menstruation, shutting off from experiencing orgasms or pleasure of any kind.

• Fear of being judged by other women in gatherings or having issues with women friends, or being in a group of women.

• Attracting failures due to the fear of being successful and being seen.

• Too scared to let go of the traditional 9-5 and pursue soul's calling.

Playing small, by not charging enough or too less for their creative gifts and services.

I am at a point in my life where I no longer hide behind my doctor credential, nor am I attached to it. I acknowledge myself that I am a doctor and much more beyond this title, a healer, whose purpose here in this life is to serve, to empower, so many other women, healers, and medicine women, who are ready to be led by their soul, who are waiting to be transformed to live their life purpefully and in alignment with the spirit.

I was shown in one of my visions when I ignite a soul by assisting in their journey of evolution. I create a ripple effect as they ignite others through their light, and this is how I rise in my consciousness, and they rise in their consciousness just like so many others who they serve.

I would be honoured if through you I get to live my soul's purpose to serve you to be seen to shine and live on your purpose, unlocking your gifts that you have brought on to this world and align with your soul's purpose of serving in your own unique way.

ABOUT THE AUTHOR

DR. FALAK SHAIKH

Dr Falak Shaikh is an Intuitive Energy Healer, a relationship coach, a best selling author of the book "The Soulmate Mantra", a wife and a mother of two beautiful kids. As a doctor of homoeopathy and an Energy Healer she has been engaging in the healing and personal transformation industry for more than 15 years. She has been helping men and women heal, grow and transform into the best versions of themselves living life in abundance aligned with soul's purpose with soulful loving relationships.

She is qualified as an MD in homoeopathy, and started her career as a doctor of Homoeopathy in India, where she was born and raised. Later in her practice she got certified in various healing modalities like Theta Healing, Reiki, EFT, Access Bars, Angel Therapy, Prana Violet Healing, Crystal Healing, Sixth Sense Healing, Ancestral Healing, Transgenerational Healing and Family Constellations. She is also an internationally certified Yoga Instructor. She is also a channel of Light Language and light codes. She has brought in the

Science and Intuitive Energy healing together to help her client heal and transform.

She now lives in Toronto, Canada with her Soulmate and beautiful kids. She says "I have been fortunate enough to create an extraordinary life for myself and I constantly work on myself, heal and grow to be the best version of myself, and I invite you to do the same in your own unique way."

Connect with Dr Falak
Website: www.falakshaiikh.com
Facebook: www.facebook.com/falak.shaikh.338
Instagram: www.instagram.com/dr_falakshaiikh/
LinkedIn: www.linkedin.com/in/falak-shaikh-92337721/

IRMA PAREDES

I AM AN EMPATH... FEELING TO FEEL DEEPLY IS MY POWER, WHAT'S YOURS?

INTRODUCTION:

"*F*eeling to FEEL Deeply is my power" gives me a unique access to see the deep hidden inner truth from myself, and today I am using its wisdom as a source of service for others to heal from within. This is something I NOW KNOW. Growing up "feeling" was too much, too painful, and too disruptive for my life and family. Being sensitive and emotional alienated me from the world and the people I loved because they didn't know HOW to be with me as I was then and as I am now.

Irma Paredes
Poet, Entrepreneur, Spiritual Coach & Leader
SOUL Connection Coaching & Events - Founder & Owner

I AM AN EMPATH... FEELING TO FEEL DEEPLY IS MY POWER, WHAT'S YOURS?

TODAY IS A NEW DAWN FOR ME.

It has taken this human life that I am now—60 years to get here. It is a beautiful cycle of life where I am finally stepping out of my ancestral binding that has held me back from powerfully stepping forward and serving with my divine gifts on Mother Earth in these unpredictable times we are living today—it is truly divine evolution.

Had I known in my childhood being sensitive, emotional, and inquisitive were spiritual gifts to be proud about would have made my life less painful than it was. Now, based on my spiritual grounding - I am grateful to have found deep peace by accepting both truths through the **SelfLove** I now honor.

Pause here - My dear reader—I want you to know that bringing this book's chapter to life has been a journey in itself. It is no surprise to experience every single moment as a singular journey, for we are endless layers upon layers of divine energy frequencies and vibrations untangling themselves to align to the next level of vibrational existence. It is us growing together in one complete experience. Now—in writing this chapter, I have gone back and forth. Light and Deep. Rewrite and Erase. Lost content to Recreate it again.

I am acutely aware of my message and everything you read here—for words are powerful. Words either 'build or destroy'. This means the story I am to share with you—its language is to be mindfully delivered, as I am sharing from the journey my Soul and I have been on.

I am an adult now—a mature adult. I am not running away from who I am, what I feel, think, or dream. I am not hiding from the little girl nor from the young woman who made her way to Toronto in 1981 creating her life through one experience after the other, unknowingly living into passages of failures and losses that eventually would deplete her strength and stop her from dreaming again—especially when it came to love and trust.

AND THERE IS ONE LIKE NONE OTHER THAN THIS ONE... MY TWIN FLAME...

We met in late October 2014 in a Latin Artist photography and poetry exhibition my mother and I attended . I was single and feeling free— new projects in the works. Life seemed to be moving well for me once again. Starting over from nothing was becoming my thing.

As people came in, I took on to greet and welcome them. Doing this was a joy. Event had begun when he came in. His way of being was intriguing to me. I silently wondered who he was here with? My curiosity got me—I wanted to know who this Asian man was. Very nonchalant, I went to him and welcomed him. He had been invited by a guest who was a NO show. He stayed. Walked about and never spoke with anyone until we found each other in a circle with others. It was interesting and uncomfortable at the same time because there was an element of enticement. I noticed his leather jacket, without thinking about it, with my right hand I reached out to his left arm and pinched the surface of the leather jacket. For some reason, I expected it to be hard leather—instead, It was soft—and I 'hum' in surprise. Neither one of us knew what to say, so we laughed. The time went on, and before ending the evening, a group picture was requested—and, yes, I made sure he was in it.

With everyone gone, I tended to my mom and packed her things; walked her to the streetcar stop on Dufferin & St. Clair St West—I made sure to go in to help her to a seat. Kisses and hugs —we said our goodnights.

Once off the streetcar, I headed home, and on the way there I was to meet with friends to celebrate the event's success. I am walking, the phone rings and I don't recognize the number. I don't answer. On the third time I give in—I say "hello" and "what?" It's him, this Asian man. I simply pinched his leather jacket for a brief trit. He is inviting me to his studio—it's close to midnight and we had just met tonight. The alluring enticing moment was long gone. I told him to call me later in the week.

His determination won me over. By the following weekend, I was in downtown Toronto to visit this alluring artist (Asian man) in his studio. It was a dinner invite. We had spoken a few times earlier in the week and based on what he shared, I was curious to be there.

He shared he is a third-generation Japanese Canadian Erotic Artist —wow!

What am I getting into?

So there I am—walking to his place—he had come out to meet me, and I thought—what a gallant gesture this was. He opened the doors for me, which impressed me and made me laugh at the same time. We got to his building, up a set of stairs to his floor, to the apartment to the door. I am nervous, and I don't know what to expect. Once he opened the door, I stepped in first. My body woke up, I took a deep breath as I was nervous for I knew I was somewhere I'd already been. The entrance is quite small, and a set of stairs led up to his studio apartment. First, he got my coat, shoes and up I went. There were a number of small paintings on the wall to my right, and I was taking it all in close to reaching the last steps taking it all in as I reached the last steps I stopped, I gasped for extra air—a painting—a small and square frame he had painted a flower that seemed to me be more of a butterfly—and the words flowed out of me so effortlessly: **I'm home** —I knew then I would never want to leave again.

The evening was divine—the music, the food, and his child-like nature, soft voice, and inquisitive eyes excited me, even though he was short—to my surprise. I had a preference for tall men—for mom always told me never to trust short men.

His whole apartment was inundated with his work, kitchen, bathroom, and balcony. The bedroom he had made his art studio, also the living room and in the middle of it -his bed- a one of a kind designed by him—it was unlike anything I had ever seen. I liked it all. It was intense and interesting. We talked, ate, danced, and joked until that moment of 'hesitation and want' occurred—we kissed which felt eternally exciting; followed with more dancing until the time to leave arrived. OMG! He went with me to the bus stop. OMG! I was over the moon joyously feeling the wonders of this experience. We shared more dates, calls, laughs and before engaging more intimately, agreements were made about our likes, conditions, and so on. Most importantly, we both agreed to get all the necessary medical tests to ensure uncompromised intimacy. I was so happy. It was a new layer of happiness.

I loved being in his space, listening to his voice as he talked about his interests. I found him to be funny—he lived naked, he was germaphobic, and he loved to cook. Indeed an artist he was. We'd meet at the Distillery and walk about for hours—I never felt bored or tired. How could I? We laughed a lot. He was/is so intricate, and for everything, he took his time, for he savoured the creation of everything and every moment..

Being with him was a haven of pleasure, colors, creativity, classical music, rich dining, and philosophical talks. My most poetic life journey began where tenderness, caring, listening, and playing were part of my everyday life experience in his space. We developed our routine, and daily conversations were deliciously engaging. We were so playful and free.

It sounds pretty incredible, doesn't it? His place eventually became home. Our weekends were all about simplicity and caring. He cared deeply, over and beyond, which I learned more about once he told me about his NOT ex-girlfriend to whom this fact was unknown. What???

Let me say it again: WHAT???

LOVE AND LOVING UNCONDITIONALLY - BECAME MY
JOURNEY.

When we met—he was dealing with the fact his girlfriend of three
years was suffering from cancer, currently in the hospital due to a
heart attack that put her in a coma. The chances for her to live were
unknown. The night he met me—he had been outside the gallery
and saw how I took care of my mother—and he knew then I was the
angel he had been looking for.

Leaving him was not a thought. However, deeper conversations led us
to become closer, and our intimacy expanded in ways I cannot write
about. What I can say is - I had never been with a more tender and
caring man as him. I had never experienced being cared for in the
ways he did care for me. He'd wash my hair and body, look after my
toes, and read to me. I wrote my poetry which he encouraged and
appreciated. And I did so while he painted to then read it out loud
later for our mutual enjoyment. He didn't have many friends, and he
lived a very simple, rich and small life which to me was a universe.

Our journey together unfolded with his NOT ex-girlfriend being part
of our journey—eventually she came out of her coma, quite weak,
her remaining time was unknown. And she now needed him. We
both understood something like this was either going to keep us
together or break us apart. This was unbearable to consider or be
with—yet, I knew I wouldn't go anywhere. They both needed me. We
talked and cried together—holding each other endlessly. We agreed
on a routine and boundaries to protect her heart and ours.

Most importantly - mine own for this I had never lived. Knowingly
and fully participating in sharing the man I love with another woman
was something I willingly had never ever done.

He was so consciously aware of her condition, and he nurtured her
soul while I nurtured his—eventually, I became part of us three.
Loving him meant loving her. So I did. I accepted what I didn't want
until it became what I could not live with—she accepted the fact I

was with him and made it clear that for her, I did not exist. Their intimate emotional connection began to affect me—feeling insecure and secondary, I felt at times I was the other woman—things began to get sour. Emotions run so deep, arguments and breaking up to return back again. We became cruel to one another, I wanted him to choose. He wanted to be alone. Until it was too much for us to handle —he wasn't going to stop visiting her—she was now dying. He pushed me away as I fought to stay. We both knew I couldn't be the angel he once sought.

He knew that I needed me far more than I needed him.

MY HEALING BEGAN...

When I understood we would not be together—my heart raptured into two.

The pain was unbearable. Between the tears and gasp for air I endured, it kept me in bed. I tried to get up, go to work or simply go outside for a walk. The flood of emotions, tears, and physical anguish depleted all my strength—all I could manage was to remain in bed and let my tears run until the flood would end.

And eventually, it did—one day, I woke up and noticed I had no more tears to cry. I got up, got some food, and realized I needed something to mark this change. I decorated the den of the apartment I was living in—got my computer and notebook. I decided I would sleep on the floor and remain there until I knew I could be out. I listened to Abraham Hicks and wrote pages and pages of things I needed to set free. After a week went by—I was finished.

I felt life return within me for me.

HEALING IN ACTIONS

A new journey opened up for me with Abraham Hicks, my daughter's spiritual friends, and my transformation. I wanted to learn more. My

soul language was back (speaking in tongues). Reiki 1 & 2. I had a
vision. A new name. Evoli and a community was born. Then, Ten
Day Vipassana Silent retreat. Ayahuasca. Mushroom ceremonies.
Sound bath meditation. Kundalini. This Evoli -energy flow of
unconditional, compassionate, universal love channeled through my
body,heart, soul and voice activated my third eye to a greater level
revealing the blockages within the physical body in people.
Everything changed. Life changed. I changed.

Created a spiritual community—lived not knowing where I'd be
living next.

I was in service and living my purpose. Toronto (uptown, downtown
and central). Oakville. Brampton. Vaughan—excited to be there. It
was a Monday morning and a new future in the making. Before going
down to the kitchen, I took a moment in my room to reflect, give
gratitude and let my soul know that this was the time for me to meet
my spiritual teacher. Computer in hand and notebook—I turned
around and stepped out of the room, went on the stairs, at the top
still I stood for a moment to take in this wonderful feeling I had. I
took my next three steps; suddenly I was slipping down the stairs so
fast I let go of everything I was holding. I looked down screaming as
my third eye showed me numbers and triangles in distance and space
—I heard a voice. In nanoseconds speed, I grabbed onto the railing to
my left as I heard my bone break. In that brief moment doing
everything my channels showed me, I knew I had saved my left leg.
My friend came to my immediate aid, helped me to a couch as I
watched my foot swelling into incredible proportions and colors. She
drove me to the nearest hospital—the x-rays showed a broken left
ankle in two places with a dislocated fibula and tibia bones. Five days
later—an operation, two screws, and a plate. In bed rest for a month
and a half. I was taking morphine for my pain. My gratitude, my trust
in the Divine and spiritual gifts took on another level as I learned to
allow others like this amazing family - take care of me.

Remember I said something about a spiritual teacher?

Well, there was a week in my recovery period that I ran out of morphine. The pain on my left foot was unbearably off chart levels. My daughter Vanessa signed me up for an alternative solution - Tao Healing program, where chanting for energy healing would support me. And it actually did, even though I did not understand it. I trusted the Divine, Vanessa, and my soul. This is how and what introduced me to the teachings of Master & Dr. Zhi Gang Sha, who today is my spiritual father and grand-master teacher.

Life continued to evolve after my fall. So did my spiritual gifts—time to create what is next.

Registered Evoli Inc.—I invited two of the community members to join me in this venture—so they did. For over six months, we met to brainstorm and develop this new company. The journey was so invigorating. I was in partnership with two powerful women I trusted fully and completely. We held work zoom meetings, assigned tasks to then meet in person where we'd discussed our findings and determined the next steps. We made agreements so clearly based on our "why" we were together embarking on our dream. One agreement was that no one would embark on any self-development courses for the current year. Well on our way in moving things forward with Evoli Inc. —we each had an area of research assigned. In this one meeting I was reporting on an area that took me about two weeks to get the appropriate information we needed. We were coming into an exciting time of our business projections. As we were about to sit down, I was pulling files out of my briefcase and I heard one of them say: "we will make it work". I looked up in wonder and said, "what are you talking about?" And this young voice from my friend replies back: "hmmm, I registered for a seven-month leadership program" with a smile upon her face. Timidly awaited for a response.

I froze—no, "this is NOT happening again" was all I was internally screaming.

She shared about her choice and so on until I asked, "when did you register?"

She replied, "two weeks ago." A cry screamed out of my heart as I dropped the files I was holding on to. What? What? Two weeks ago? And you are telling me now? I have been working on this and that, etc. I was in shock, to say the least. My heart ached. I felt betrayed all over again! That day marked the end of Evoli Inc., and also a part of me.

The impact and effect on our friendship was deep. She was soon to step into a leadership training program with great support in place. While I was left to process the impact of it all on my own. Once again — I had nothing. As the three of us moved on into our separate paths, there was such emotional pain within me that I needed more time to process it. A blessing that made the difference is that we were both highly transformed human beings—yes, we both were and upon mutual agreement we embarked on a journey to continue talking this experience out until there was nothing more to say about it.

Hopefully till there was no more pain.

It took over a year and a half for me to reach complete peace and forgiveness. And every time a new layer of self-discovery on my part showed up, I'd call her and share until one day I realized the success of Evoli Inc. was never dependent on her. It was dependent on me. And, yes, I did call her to share that too -setting her free was our gift to each other.

This marked the beginning of something deeper being healed for me because I discovered - that none of it had been personal. What a delicious breakthrough for me and my existence.

Life continued to evolve, unfold, and I found new projects to engage in.

And an old enquiry showed up in my space once again. Why have I needed to be *'seen, heard, accepted and included'* as I have? Where did this begin? Why is it still showing up in me? It hurts when it does, it's time to make peace with me. I didn't want to continue living inside the pain of these unanswered questions.

I am now a Tao Hands Practitioner Healer, business owner- Soul Connection Coaching & Events. I live alone and in my own place. Learning, adapting, and integrating the Tao Chang and Master Sha's teaching and wisdom—has purified and uplifted my spiritual gifts in ways that go beyond what human beings know about energy healing. I am beyond grateful. I am also in a training program for my ongoing growth and development as a human being.

Why I am sharing this with you now, you may ask my dear reader, it's because I want you to know I am healing my emotional human suffering in this lifetime so it doesn't have to be in the next one.

LET'S STEP BACK ... A VALUABLE ACT OF SELFLOVE

Growing up, I heard my mom many times share the story of HOW she came to learn she was pregnant a fourth time. She was breastfeeding one child of her own, plus other babies from our neighbourhood in Cerro La Cruz, Chile. She noticed she wasn't feeling well for a bit, so she went to see her doctor about it. After his examination, he tells her she is seven months pregnant. Two months later, I was born.

As I mentioned earlier—I am looking for answers to this deeply rooted need of mine that wants to know so desperately WHY I need to be seen, heard, accepted, and included?

Why does it torment me? Why is it so personal? Why? It hurts so much when I am rejected, betrayed, denied, excluded, and so much more.

REMEMBER - FEELING TO FEEL DEEPLY IS MY POWER.

I am working at my desk at home - my environment is based on love, tranquility and peace.

I feel a sensation of a gentle wave moving through within me, and outside of me. I wonder 'what is this?' - I ask out loud as I get myself up and away from my desk. I begin to see images and words, letters. I stop moving. I close my eyes. My third eye fully open and activated, I immediately began to experience 'my seeing' myself during the seven months my mother didn't know I even existed?! I was very still, head down and unnoticeably growing. There was a faint layer of "LIGHT" covering me. It felt so warm. Outside of me -there was a world of feelings, emotions and activities. None though were the loving whispers a mother does over her tummy. No gentle touching to connect with this being: me. No awareness. No excitement about my existence or future arrival. What did I actually absorb through her womb in those months I presumably didn't exist? As I am 'seeing through my third eye' these images, I find that I am actually curious at this moment about her —my mother, what did she feel? What did she first think? What were her first words to me? Without asking anything, I know there must have been—shock, surprise and concerns. She was, after all, a twenty years old young married woman. Already a mother of three, and now me.

I heard myself breathe deeply and tears began to flow as I stood still for a little while. I opened my eyes, lit some candles and did nothing for the rest of that day. I felt such inner peace that I chose to simply HONOR IT. My mother is still alive, due to old age and health conditions she is unable to engage in this kind of conversation that I would have liked to have with her.

And truth be told, I actually feel quite alright about it all—for I am not afraid to "Feeling—to FEEL deeply" what I am to find out on my own. I have my gifts. I am already free from within.

IN MY PRESENT NOW I FLOURISH BECAUSE...

Over the years I have heard again and again that I am the creator of my own life. And I am. As I look back at each one of these life experiences, I can see with clarity and ownership that each embodied an invincible component known as "betrayal" that made me a self-victim of/to my own need to be "seen, heard, felt and included". The power of this Inner Truth reveals to me that "**Betrayal**" is my own assumed perception.

I now live free from within to love myself as deeply as I can possibly infinitely love thee...Me!

ABOUT THE AUTHOR

IRMA PAREDES

Irma Paredes calling in serving humanity is about LOVE. She is here to INSPIRE you to open up your heart, mind, body and soul; step into a journey of **SelfLove** that EMPOWERS you to explore more deeply your power to end your own human suffering.

Irma's **SelfLove** Journey unfolded through life's experiences that brought her to where she is now by unmasking negative polarities that blocked "loving me" from herself. As a COACH and HEALER today Irma can compassionately guide - mentor - coach those who want to unmask their own polarities and make peace with all their parts of Self, Soul and Humanity.

SelfLove it's a Journey to Embody Your Undeniable Brilliance!

The **SelfLove** Journey requires an open mind, heart and strong willingness to step into the unknown of self. To support her clients, she discovered the best process is embodying BEING a 'safe and trusting space through her LISTENING' that naturally opens the space for what the client needs.

SOUL Connections Coaching methodology is based on THREE components:

Guidance - Mentorship - Coaching within FOUR conversations, FOUR distinctions, and THREE conversational structures that are supported through Spiritual guidance (Tao Hands practices and meditations). Awakening the Heart - Membership based Monthly Community Gathering. SOUL Connection Coaching & Events offers: Group or 1 ON 1 packaged sessions. Flagship workshop: Love Letter to Self - One day event; Thirty Days **SelfLove** Journey program. In 2022 introducing "Feeling to Feel Deeply" A **SelfLove** three and half month program that includes utero trauma healing.

Irma Paredes was born in Chile and has resided in Canada since Jan 25, 1975.

She moved from Sarnia in 1981 to Toronto making it her permanent home. Married and divorced twice - best part of both -her most precious gems: Leonardo (Son) Maison(Grandson) Catarina & Vanessa (Daughters)

Connect with Irma:

Facebook: www.facebook.com/SoulConnectionCoaching

Instagram: www.instagram.com/soulconnectioncoaching/

LinkedIn: www.linkedin.com/in/irma-paredes-64b13527

LYSA GYLEN

TRANSFORMING SUBCONSCIOUS LIMITING BELIEFS TO FIND FREEDOM WITHIN

INTRODUCTION:

"*W*hen was the last time you truly felt fulfilled?" Divine whispered.

You had to think about this one. It's been a while since you've connected with that feeling. You've been so busy being busy that you've had no time to pause and listen to yourself.

You've been so afraid to face yourself that you kept going, and doing, and running to the next new thing. As long as you're busy, you don't need to face YOU, the real you!

Divine whispered again: "Take a deep breath in, hold it. I've got you! Hold! And exhale! Take a moment to ask yourself..."

What would you like to change about your life?

What does it cost you not to make a change?

What's the worst thing that would happen if you manifested everything you wanted?

You know you're here to do something meaningful, but you don't know what.

You're fed up trying to figure things out.

You are here to find your purpose but you feel so lost.

You have no idea who you are anymore or what to do next.

I was there too!

What if you can shift your energetic state of being to have more joy, infinite possibilities, and embody the new version of yourself?

What would your life look like, feel like if you've found your life purpose, your inner confidence, and love for who you are?

I'm here to show you how to transform subconscious limiting beliefs into empowering patterns and tap into the powers of your body, your intuition, and your purpose.

> Trust yourself.
> Connect with yourself.
> You are all you need.
> You can do this.
> You are safe to be seen.
> Earth supports you.
> You can THRIVE on Earth.

Lysa (lai-sa) Gylen
Certified Advanced Theta Healer
Tao Hands Practitioner Certified by the Tao Academy
Quantum Flow Practitioner

WHAT WE ATTRACT IS A CONFIRMATION OF WHAT WE BELIEVE

Late evening. I didn't expect this. It's the first time he hit me in my face. I landed on the bed. My chin hurts; I can hardly move my head. When I did, he had already left the bedroom. The smell of alcohol, tobacco, and Paco Rabanne was still lingering in the air. I looked in the mirror, and my lip was split, blood was streaming down the chin. My body was shaking, going into survival mode. It's exhausting to live in fear and anxiety.

I want to be back in the womb. Ohh, hold on, I don't think it felt safe there either. When my mother was pregnant with me, she was dealing with an alcoholic husband and under a lot of stress. I absorbed the pain caused by her constant quarrels and disappointments. She was emotionally shattered. Energetically, I didn't feel nurtured because she was also preoccupied with my one-year-old sister, work and was pretty much "out-of-body" during her pregnancy. I felt as if I was holding space for her! It was heavy. I didn't want to be born; it wasn't safe to come to Earth, too dark and dense here. The contrast between the higher state and the lower 3D state - horrendous - felt like death. I couldn't plug in here on Earth. I didn't feel welcome.

Back to the split lip, blood was streaming down my chin, another wound. I took a quick picture of my face. I couldn't call anyone that night, not even my mother. We've not spoken for many months. I was ashamed to tell her that my relationship was falling apart and that, once again, she was correct with her predictions.

I was so angry at myself. If I had listened to my mum's warning, this wouldn't happen. At the same time, I probably wouldn't explore the world and what life had to offer outside of my comfort zone. I know I made the right choice at the time, or maybe the choice I made was to make my mum upset. To prove to her that I can have a strong union with a man and not repeat the family pattern of broken marriages.

Maybe I made that choice because I was angry at her for taking my diary without my permission. Maybe I made that choice because she put me under house arrest after reading my diary. I felt trapped at home. All I could control was what I ate. I felt so misunderstood.

I moved in with him three months after we met. We bonded very quickly, and I followed my heart, really wanting to make it work. Now, it's a seven-year itch. Times have changed, and so has his personality. From a man who was kind, loving, generous, he turned into aggressive and abusive. This relationship was mentally and emotionally challenging. He would be verbally abusive, making me feel small just to make himself feel better. Our spending habits were different. We would fight about him not paying into a joint account and not having enough left at the end of the month. I couldn't get on a property ladder with him.

The last time I told him I was leaving him, he threatened to set my grandma's house on fire and kill my family. That scared me, so I stayed because I didn't think I was worthy of anything better. I felt caged. However, this time around, it was different. I kept repeating to myself, "I am strong, I am strong. I can do it." I can plan an escape without saying a word. I just want my family to be safe.

I knew I was living with a narcissist, but I didn't do anything to leave him. They say love is blind, and maybe the abuse was my definition of love as all I've witnessed and heard was my mother being beaten by my dad first and then by my stepdad. The latter hit her so bad that she had to have her arm in a cast for two months. And what children do–we learn about love through observing our parents.

WE REPEAT WHAT WE DON'T REPAIR

I didn't know my biological father as mum left him when I was a year old. He was an engineer by trade, had a drinking problem, and was physically and verbally abusive towards her. She was a hardworking medical doctor with two kids. I came here second. Always second. I heard stories about him and how he would invite women home whilst mum was at work. One day she caught him, and the rest was history.

Finally, I felt empowered to leave him. I was also terrified at the same time. I found a local YMCA that offered me an emergency room to stay. The building was security protected, so I'd be safe. A few days later, we were both getting ready for work. As soon as he left the house, I packed my suitcase with essentials and a desire to be free.

I changed my phone number so he wouldn't get hold of me. However, the day after my move, he was outside of my work crying and asking me to come back. There was no way I would go back. Every day, he would wait for me to finish work and follow me in his car. He had no idea where I moved.

I worked as an Accounting Technician in Windsor, and most days, I would leave work early enough so that he wouldn't follow me. Most evenings, I would spend with my girlfriends, talking things through and planning my next steps. It made me scared seeing him driving around the town looking for me, and one day he was outside my work as my colleague and I were heading out to have lunch. After I refused to talk to him, he grabbed me by my neck. I screamed—déjà vu. I had a flashback. When I was a child, I dreamt a lot about past lives, abusive marriage, hands on my throat, silenced, fear around speech. Violence against women has a long history, and this deep-rooted trauma was recorded in me.

By the time my colleague called the police, he was already gone. The police visited me later that day, asking tons of questions. The same day, he was issued a restraining order. That was it. Now, I had to run far from him, closing this chapter of my life and focusing on me.

WE REPEAT WHAT'S FAMILIAR

We repeat the beliefs, behaviour patterns, coping skills that we learnt in childhood when we were vulnerable, and our brains weren't fully developed. And after years of repeating the same pattern, they are hard to break.

Coming out of an abusive relationship felt like my angel wings were broken, my self-esteem was super low, and now I also had to build up a healthy sense of worth, learning to love myself for who I am. Back then, I didn't know that I could transform negative beliefs about myself as well as my state of being!

I was terrified of falling back into the emptiness and loneliness that I had experienced before I met him. But what I've had, up until this point, hadn't felt like life.

With heaviness around my heart, I found that spending time with old friends in the clubs of London, drinking Jager Bombs, dancing till the sunrise on a beach of Brighton, and experimenting with psychedelics was the best therapy for me at the time. I've found my escape, and it felt great. I was constantly meeting new people, numbing out the pain with alcohol, and ignoring the inner voice that was longing for deep healing.

RELATIONSHIP WITH FOOD

Soon, I started feeling anxious about going out and kept myself to myself. After the breakup, I was looking for comfort to fill this void inside my heart. Emotional eating was something new to me. I've never been a great eater. After a battle with anorexia, I've kept restrictive eating for as long as I can remember, surviving on up to eight hundred calories a day.

This time, it was different. I felt the pull to stuff myself, to fill that emotional need. I had no control over it. It manifested by me running away from negative emotions and memories. It was as if someone was pulling me on a string to a supermarket. Having been restricting food for so long, my stomach couldn't digest food quickly anymore. It would swell up so much that everything I ate had to come back up. It made me feel worse. The back of my throat was very sore from purging. Every time I purged, I would sob. It was suffocating. I beat myself with judgement, shame, and guilt and considered *that* as normal. I believed that there was something wrong with me. In so many ways, I was aggressive and disrespectful of my body and feelings and how I loved myself was how I taught others to love me.

I remember when I was little, I refused to eat certain foods, especially red meat. I was told to eat everything on my plate. I had a little round bag that I would wear across my body and hide food inside when mum turned around.

I've always admired my mum for how beautiful she was. On the weekends, I watched her exercising on the floor. She would hide sweets from us on the top shelf of the living room cabinet and only gave us sweets on Sundays.

My sugar cravings were unbearable. I remember at the age of four, my mum and sister took me to a supermarket. I ran away straight to the sweets department by the entrance, grabbed a bag with toffees off the shelf, and started eating them in the corner. A female shopkeeper grabbed me from my hood, "whose child is this?" she shouted. My mum and sister came rushing from the other side of the supermarket, giving me evil looks. I was missing the sweetness of life.

GRANDDAD'S AND DAD'S DEATH

Mum was working two jobs so that we could have a nice home and summer holidays away. Sometimes, I'd be sent to my grandparents, where I'd spend time with my cousins. That summer was special, and my granddad decided to "fall asleep" for good. The cousins and I just came back from picking sweet peas in the field as we saw mum running towards us. I didn't know she was coming to get me today. She took my hand and quietly said that grandad is resting on the kitchen floor, and he doesn't want to be disturbed. I have seen many relatives "falling asleep" including my dad, who passed away from cancer. Attending burial services and visiting relatives in a cemetery didn't freak me out anymore, but I didn't like it. It was something I've learnt to accept as part of life. I now know that the soul is eternal, and it houses in the body. No one knows how long we have here on Earth, unless you're psychic. All we can do is nurture the home of our soul. I didn't know at the time what this would even look like.

WOUNDING OF THE FEMININE

My mum's love languages are 'acts of service' and 'receiving gifts'. And what I wanted was quality time with her and physical touch, not the hard tapping on my back as she often did, but a soft tender hug. This girl wanted to be lovingly held. Mum wouldn't use words such as 'love' to tell me she loved me, but I felt her love in every meal she cooked, and everything she bought for me was filled with love.

When my mum was little, she experienced a hard upbringing, which left her feeling alone throughout her childhood. Her mother was physically there, but emotionally unavailable. Did you know that we receive aspects of our grandmother's mothering through our mother, including trauma, pain, and challenges in childhood?

When growing up, I wanted to be mum's good girl. As soon as I was able to, I would help tidy the house, dust shelves, and I would do anything for her love. But I knew I would never be her number one as my older sister had already taken that place. No matter how hard I tried to build an emotional connection with mum, I didn't feel good enough. I was compared to my sister all the time. We were different and I felt I didn't fit in, not at home, nor school. Later on in life, when I started doing belief work with ThetaHealing, I uncovered that I held subconscious limiting beliefs that "I'm a mistake," and "I'm damaged". These beliefs can create obstacles in our life, especially when we want to move from a comfort zone into a stretch zone.

My sister and I tried to get on, but our interaction always ended up in tears. It was a similar pattern in my grandma's family. We were not taught how to express our emotions that would support our development, just told to be quiet, sit in the corner, sort ourselves out. The only time my sister and I bonded well and had fun was when we both played the piano and mum sang. These were our happy family times, no competition, just music.

I ended up with pneumonia at the age of six. Even though I got to meet many cool kids at the hospital, I felt alone. Mum was working a lot, dad didn't want to know me, and I felt abandoned by God. Does God even exist?—I asked. This feeling was getting me down. I didn't feel worthy of love.

Later on, I came to understand that my parents had their own trauma, and it was their trauma that blocked the love they were able to give. Understanding this opened me up for more compassion for them and what I experienced as a result of being their daughter.

UNTIL WE LEARN TO HEAL THE WOUNDS WE'VE HAD SINCE CHILDHOOD, WE WILL CONTINUE TO REPEAT THE SAME PATTERNS UNTIL WE DO

I went through a rollercoaster with restrictive eating, constantly getting dizzy spells, becoming easily tired, and ended up with anemia. And even then, I didn't start eating more. "I am fine," I kept telling myself! The disappearance of periods didn't alarm me either. I was quite happy not to have them as when I had them, I was in bed in agony. When my hair started falling out, my skin got dryer and dryer, and my nails became brittle, I thought I could do something about it by slapping some oil on the skin. So, I went to a supermarket to get some oil, feeling incredibly cold and dizzy, and the next thing I knew, I was lying on the floor with paramedics breathing down my face. I guess that's my wake-up call. On the way to the hospital, my head was filled with confusion, loss, and heartbreak. It's all my fault, never going to heal this wound. Earth is cruel, doesn't support me. I just want to sleep.

The anger I felt turned inward and suppressed. Instead of telling people about my worries, I chose to say nothing and take anger out on my eating. I just didn't know how to verbalise my feelings, express emotions, or confront problems. It was getting me down. I developed an obsessive-compulsive disorder. I became obsessed with tidiness—cups and glasses arranged in order of height, toiletries faced the same way, etc. I became anxious about germs, washed my hands endlessly, and I couldn't leave the house without going around tightening all the taps first. I was worried about walking on the cracks in the pavement. Then, I ran back home to ensure the front door was properly locked, and every time I went back, the door was locked.

At the time, I was working as a Business Manager for a luxury brand and very quickly progressed to a District Manager's role, and thanks to OCD, I won several awards for the best operational standards. I loved what I did at the time, and it allowed me to travel across the UK, meet inspiring people, visit new cities and see architecture.

I got into personal development and listened to audiobooks on the way to and from work. I was inspired by attending seminars on various topics and really invested in myself. I even went backpacking in Canada to take part in Robin Sharma's workshops, and whilst there, I visited Niagara Falls. I'd get up at 5 am to do my guided meditation, followed by affirmations and an exercise routine. I've never liked journaling. Writing wasn't my favourite thing in the world. I was diagnosed with dyslexia and ADHD, and I used them as an excuse not to write. However, I've always been a number-crunching person who loves Excel sheets, so I was very happy to deal with sales reports, trackers, and budgeting.

I had a distorted idea of my body image. Exercise played an integral part in my life, and like everything else, it turned into compulsive exercising. I was never happy with my body and always sought to increase the length of my cardio sessions. The more I was losing weight, the more I wanted to lose, the less I ate, which led me, now I know it, to be depressed.

I restricted food intake in the belief that it would improve my physical appearance. It was not until years later, when I hired a Personal Trainer and educated myself on nutrition, I realised that food doesn't make me fat, it's the beliefs, and the meaning I give to food that makes it appear so.

"Emotion is the doorway to your body!" ~Juan Pablo Barahona

I was looking for a purpose in life but didn't quite know how to connect to it. When I was offered a job as a Business Manager in Toronto, I was over the moon. The only thing I didn't know was that I'd be struggling with health challenges and self-care. My challenges came because it was hard for me to know how to prioritise and meet all the needs. I was overwhelmed and blamed myself for the struggle, seeing the struggle as a sign that, again, there was something wrong with me. And so life was presenting me with more people and circumstances that validated this for me.

A year later, I had burned out. I felt like my energy was sucked out of me, I was drained and depressed. I had no energy to pretend that everything was fine and pull the mask on with a permanent smile on my face! My world was crashing down, and I needed to be honest with myself. I was struggling to cope. I had physical symptoms that reflected emotional and psychological issues. Most of it came from my mindset of fight or flight that potentially was creating a dis-ease and disharmony in the body. My nervous system needed a full reset.

"You don't find light by avoiding the darkness" ~ S. Kelley Harrell

---

With a trusted psychotherapist, I went on a journey of deep healing to the jungle of the Amazon. I connected to nature like I had never connected before, singing around the fire, sleeping under the stars in a hammock and of course getting bitten by mosquitoes. I prayed for guidance, peace, and healing. The first night I was there during the ceremony, I experienced what felt like death and rebirth. I could feel a huge veil was lifted off, the energy around my heart was spiralling, and it felt as though more space was created for me to breathe. "Breathe deeply, breathe into your heart", the voice whispered. My heart felt lighter, and my body surrendered fully and completely, allowing the plant medicine to nurture and heal me.

I started letting go of everything I thought I should be, the identity, the titles in order to be worthy of love. There was a longing to parent my inner child and reassure her that she is safe in her body, always connected to and supported by the Earth.

Now, I'm in a safe and loving womb of Mother Earth. For the first time in my life, I was able to energetically sink into the Earth, feeling calm and relaxed.

I belong here. I am enough! I am exactly where I need to be!

And I trust. I trust life. I see medicine in all my difficulties.

"Awakening is not changing who you are but disregarding who you are not" ~ Deepak Chopra

I questioned myself: How could hating and punishing my body have ever felt good to me? All those years of being at war with my body haven't helped me. I was fighting the same old battle, still criticising myself, which brought me more of the same. I had to bring awareness to the problem, take time to reflect, sit with myself, with my body, and learn to forgive myself. I was forgiving myself for all self-hatred, for being trapped in pain and self-loathing. I've found that I can work through the discomfort and deep pain by feeling *compassion* towards myself. To have a truly compassionate relationship with myself, meant to embrace and accept myself unconditionally, so that I can fully heal. Full *self-acceptance* was a huge step for me. Accepting meant not fighting or resisting the reality, but *being at peace* with what is.

Through daily forgiveness practices and *being raw and real* with myself, I was learning body whispering, developing a dialogue with my body, asking what it needs and listening for the answers. Initially, it felt weird talking to the body, but the more I did it, the more I heard and felt the answers my body conveyed. It was very emotional. I was consistent with the body whispering, and felt at peace with myself, and what I noticed was the eczema I've had for years started to disappear.

FINDING MY TRUE SELF WITHIN

My healing journey gave me an awareness that *I AM a Soul* in a human body. I was guided to attend an Aquarian Teacher Training to deepen my experience of Kundalini Yoga and my Soul Body, the "inner self". When our connection to our Soul Body is weak, it'll be harder to find the strength to live our passions and follow our bliss. We'll get stuck in "what-ifs". When our Soul Body is strong and powerful, we live a creative life full of purpose. We live from our heart and feel infinitely loved by the flow of the Universe.

Kundalini Yoga led me to sound healing, then work as an Ayurvedic massage therapist and an intuitive energy healer. I had a desire to learn about human psychology, so I went back to university to study that. The most transformational healing I've experienced was subconscious reprogramming and Soul work, all based on science, which I use in my work with clients and my daily practices.

Belief is the acceptance of the mind that something is true, often underpinned by the emotional sense of certainty. ~Steve Sisgold

I found ThetaHealing® when I was at a lowest point in my life. I lived in a black hole for so long that I had no idea how to live without sadness and anxiety. I had resistance to happiness and my health. I tended to blame my parents for the way I was. At the time, I found my family controlling and developed anorexia as a last stand to maintain my own power. Most of my beliefs were related to how others saw me and the way I felt about myself and life. Once I cleared the emotional blocks, I was free to own my power without the need to recreate mental health challenges.

Our body reacts to the emotional belief systems to which it is conditioned. The key is to change the messages that are sent to the body and to do that, we have to change the beliefs. The research done by Dr. Candace Pert, the author of "Molecules of Emotions", indicates that "there is a communication between human mind and cells. The neuropeptides and immunopeptides are the messengers of this communication. The emotions experienced can directly impact the cells in the body either causing disease or keeping cells in the state of health"[1].

"Heal the Soul first; then healing of the mind and body will follow" ~
Dr and Master Sha

During my healing journey, I've received a Tao Hands light transmission from the beloved teacher Dr. and Master Zhi Gang Sha and have been using Tao Technology to transform blockages in the electromagnetic field to create harmony in the body. Since using my Tao Healing Hands, my sense of self-worth has increased, and my relationship with my mother has transformed dramatically. Areas of the relationship that triggered us before seem to flow effortlessly. Where we both overreacted before or struggled to communicate, we now respond with grace and ease and have an open conversation. I'm beyond grateful!

Through the powerful forgiveness practices of the Tao, I've worked on healing my mother and father wounds. Even though I never knew my father, I was connected to him through quantum entanglement, subconsciously held his negative beliefs and repeated his patterns. I needed to heal my relationship with my parents and transform negative information and vibrations of judgement, anger, pain, fear, scarcity that I've been carrying in my field, my body, cells all the way to the DNA and RNA.

Tao practices include invocations, chanting, calligraphy tracing and so much more, and for me they hold the key to personal transformation on all levels. In order to heal, we need to heal the Soul first.

"The best way to move forward is to let go of what's holding you back" ~Juan Pablo Barahona

The next upgrade I received was during the Quantum Flow Certification with Juan Pa Barahona. The embodiment practices quickly shifted my energetic state, from being depressed to feeling alive and awake again. Both hemispheres of my brain, feminine and masculine, became balanced and my whole nervous system, where much of the stuck energy resides, was rewired.

As a result of doing inner work, the eating disorders and sugar cravings I've had for years were completely gone! My love for life and love for myself was awakened, making me feel empowered, confident, and more genuinely compassionate towards myself and others. The love of another person doesn't define me, nor does it define my value as a person. Because I know how to embody love in every cell of my being. I AM LOVE.

This is why we call it 'inner work'. We generate energy internally, working through the body from a deep cellular level, bio-hacking the nervous system, upgrading electromagnetic field, and tapping into the messages of the Soul—the inner guidance. So that no matter what happens externally, and no matter what's taken away from us, we're not affected internally.

We're 99.99% energy, and energy is the space of infinite creation. We're a vehicle of energy, and our electromagnetic frequency is affecting that which we're manifesting in our life. Our energy is heavily influenced by our time in the womb. Every time we're triggered by a wound, we're creating a pattern in our life that gets repeated until we deal with the trigger. All of it is connected to the subconscious mind and related to the nervous system.

Our nervous system is affected by our thoughts and emotions. Did you know that our thoughts are electric and emotions magnetic? When we connect electric and magnetic together, the mind and the heart, we get an electromagnetic frequency (EMF) or a field that surrounds us. It's the signal that emanates from the core of our being. The EMF attracts things, people, circumstances, and energy to us. Everything has an energetic connection. Another reason why we must commit to having higher-level thinking, connecting to gratitude and becoming aware of how we feel, what we say, how we treat others because all of this affects our field.

The body is our vehicle for manifestation, and if we tune our vehicle with high-level thoughts, beliefs, positive spoken language, high vibrational food, exercise, fresh air, clean water, we're bringing the vibration up, and the signal that we're broadcasting will reflect that.

Negative emotions can and do get stuck as crystallised energy in the nervous system and this energy holds information about our wounds. We can transform stuck energy into the energy of creation through the alchemy process where crystallised energy shifts into the energy of infinite potential. We go deep into the electric currents of the nervous system and burn the blind spots to create space for the new intention we choose to embody. When we commit to doing the inner work, we're bringing in the new programs we want to create in our life. This is how we create a new vibration, new patterns that have a ripple effect on seven generations back and seven generations forward.

If you ever feel resistant to doing the inner work, this is a sign you need to start doing it! The ego is addicted to suffering and it will resist because it wants to keep you safe. If you fight the ego - you feed the ego. The best way to approach it is to become an observer of the current reality and be grateful for what is showing up. See thoughts as passing clouds, without getting attached to them. When emotions come up, acknowledge them, feel them but don't feed them. Being aware of, and detached from old negative patterns, without controlling them, will open doors to Quantum reality so that you can live the life you want to create. Creation is not all about us, we're constantly co-creating with the Quantum Field. All we need to do is, get out of the way, by revealing our blind spots.

When I transformed low-vibration emotions into high-level frequencies, I awakened my soul purpose. Every time I do my flow, I'm bringing my body back to its natural state, which is the vibration of the soul. As I do my flow, I dance in spirals, the movement of nature and the cosmos. I surrender and take time to integrate what I've just called in. I AM LOVE. I'm connected with my soul, aligned with the cosmos, and living in Divine Truth. I've worked on physical, energetic, mental, emotional, and spiritual levels simultaneously. My heart is overflowing with love. I arrived home. I am at home in my body. I've experienced trust in myself, trust in God, and that unshakable *inner confidence*. I no longer need to look for validation outside of myself. All I need is inside of me. I AM. I AM. I AM whatever I choose to BE.

These life-transforming healing modalities have supported me, and my clients to move through challenges, resistance, and uncertainty. I bring people the ability to release, let go, to create space in the body in order to heal and find freedom within.

I thank you for being on this journey with me!

This is an invitation for you to expand, evolve, and step into the beautiful life you deserve.

You absolutely can have freedom within!

With Love, Peace & Harmony,

Your Guide,

Lysa (lai-sa)

---

1. Pradhan, A. (2017). Homeopathy–Nanomedicine-Mechanism of Action of Homeopathic Medicines.

ABOUT THE AUTHOR

LYSA GYLEN

Lysa Gylen (lai-sa) is a Certified Advanced Theta Healer, Tao Hands Practitioner, and a Quantum Flow Practitioner.

Through an intuitive blend of these modalities, Lysa supports women who feel held back by limitations to find confidence and reclaim freedom within.

Lysa's path into this work wasn't an easy one, but every experience in her life has enabled her to serve her clients on the deepest possible level.

After struggling with disordered eating and mental health problems for 25 years, Lysa knows how impossible it can feel to even *imagine* a way out of your personal darkness.

It is her greatest service in life to support other women who are struggling to feel empowered, find their way out of their own darkness, and back into their true selves within.

Connect with Lysa
Website: www.lysagylen.com/
Instagram: www.instagram.com/lysagylen/
Facebook: www.facebook.com/LysaGylen/

RACHEL ANNE WATKINS

FREE TO LIVE YOUR RICH AUTHENTICALLY ALIGNED, WHOLESOME LIFE

INTRODUCTION:

*A*re you growing weary from pleasing everyone in your life at the sacrifice of yourself? Are you beginning to feel the impact your lifestyle has on all levels of body, mind, and spirit? Are symptoms popping up out of nowhere? Does it feel as though you are stuck?

In your heart, you carry a deep knowing the time is now. It is time to stop, time for a change, time for growth and time for expansion and to live the life you've always dreamed of. But—it is so damn scary. You know what to do, but consistency is hard. Life is hard. Facing judgment and criticism is hard.

Oh my friend, you are stronger than you know. I am here to be your support, your rock, your biggest cheerleader, your strength on the toughest of days.

When I stopped, my story began. By creating necessary changes for myself, I lost what I thought was the worst thing in life to lose: my parents. Little did I know losing what I held most precious and dear would allow me to find something more profound than I ever thought imaginable. I found myself, my essence, my core, my Dharma, my SOUL. My brave spirit allowed me to step out of fear and into faith through consistent practice of using awareness and knowledge to strengthen my body and mind. When I said yes to myself and healing my body, my mind, and my spirit, I also said yes to my life.

Dear friend, I tell you with sincerity, honesty, and love you are going to be fine. You will move to the other side of all that which is weighing you down and into alignment—you will feel fucking amazing! When the waves of life have tossed you around, and you have lost your way, look for the light. Your journey begins here.

With over 15 years of experience in my field of passion and expertise, health and wellness, I have learned the secret recipe for restoring harmony in the body, mind, and spirit, and I am so excited to share it with you.

Heal yourself, heal the world.

Rachel Anne Watkins
Intuitive and Holistic Health Guide, Tarot Reader, and Yoga Instructor

FREE TO LIVE YOUR RICH, AUTHENTICALLY ALIGNED, WHOLESOME LIFE

"Rachel, you are leaving on Friday. Are you packed?"

Knowing I was getting to visit him filled me with such anticipation that I would hold my breath. So desperately desiring that it would actually be him to pick me up this time.

I looked up to my parents so much. I craved their love with everything in my being, as all children do.

My parents were merely children themselves when they had me. With only twenty years between us, we were all growing in our own way. They were still discovering more about themselves and who they were. I was discovering and learning this 3D Earth I just reincarnated into.

For seven years, I was an only child and played the role well. It was all about me. I was the center of my mom's world, something to draw my dad's attention to, and the apple of my paternal grandmother's eye. I felt so special, so loved.

As luck would find it, I found myself alone, often, which was wonderful as it aligns with my astrology blueprint. This allowed me to become the watchful "seer." I was really good at feeling the energy of those around me at a very young age.

I learned early on how to operate depending on what parent I was with. Unspoken agreements were made between us. One thing that was the same no matter who I was with was that keeping the peace and everyone happy was the priority. I did my best to be seen and not heard.

I worked hard, got good grades, followed directions, and would stand at attention waiting to find what I could do next to keep the waters calm. If I only knew, we don't have the power to control anybody else's water but our own.

I would expend much of my energy seeking validation that I was doing a good job. Validation and compliments were not doled out very often, so when they came, I was able to exhale, but only for a little bit. Then, back to holding my breath and externally searching outside of myself for validation and, sadly, acceptance.

My family eventually grew, and I found myself having to shift gears, to play a new role. I was the oldest sister of four girls. With each new sibling, it seemed to tweak my role just a bit. I was always looking for that sweet spot where I was helpful but still maintained my position with both of my parents. Keep the peace, be ready to jump, and wait for the validation—that was love.

My parents divorced when I was very young. There are many things I do not recall growing up, but what I do remember was this.

I, for the most part, lived with my mother. She was strong, independent, smart, wise, dedicated, and loving. As challenging as being a single parent can be, she did it with ease and grace, from my perspective. Of course, she had her moments and would break down, but I was on the ready to help her where I could. She always got through, and these moments made me admire her strength and ability to keep stability. She was a true badass!

What I remember most was how she prioritized my sister and I. Above all else.

For example, we were always enrolled in a private school, which I am grateful for. The opportunity to experience this type of education set me up with a good moral compass. I enjoyed having the checklist, Commandments, to use when I wanted to make sure I was doing a good job. However, some of its teachings left me with some questions.

Despite being the "good girl" with my parents, I have always been very curious. If something didn't make sense to me, I would question it.

Not with my parents, of course, that would be catastrophic. However, questioning my teachers and religious leaders was where I tested the waters of stepping outside of the box. This was not well received but was safe because there was no risk of losing anyone or anything.

My mom loved filling our childhood with adventures and creating memories. We took many camping, skiing, and road trips. She did such a beautiful job of showing us the beauty this earth holds while teaching us to continue to be curious and never stop exploring. This instilled a love and passion for nature into me.

I remember being part of the process for many things, going to the grocery store, having her teach me how to know when the grapes are good to buy and how to find the best deals. Enrolling me for certain chores, dishes mostly, being part of the checkbook balancing process and letting me know that there were certain things we could not afford. She was an amazing teacher, even in my teenage years when I'd roll my eyes when she would offer the lesson.

She supported and loved me unconditionally. She made it a point to be at my volleyball and basketball games, wearing my pin, and at times cheering so loudly it was almost embarrassing. I loved it though, having my own cheer squad, believing in me when it felt like no one else was.

There are only a few distinct memories of my father from my younger years. My parents lived four hours apart, eight hours round trip. I have nearly every curve, stop, and landmark etched into my memory. I could drive it with my eyes closed.

When the day arrived to go to my dad's, I would be filled with so much anticipation and hope. Hoping I would get to see him more than I did last time. I would also think, "Maybe it will even be him to pick me up this time. I know he said [another person] was going to get me, but maybe he will surprise me. Oh, that would be so amazing."

My dad was a hard-working American farmer who was determined to build a better life for himself and his family. Farming requires time, and lots of it, no matter the season. Therefore, work did not stop because it was Thanksgiving, Christmas, Easter, or because I was there. This meant our time together was very limited, which created a deep desire to be with him as much as possible. I watched my dad live his life through which I learned how to work hard, be strong, tough, and do it all, whatever it was, without complaint. One unique agreement I took on with him was never to show emotion, especially difficult emotions. Again, I learned to follow the rules, be the good girl, and keep the peace, so our time together was joyful.

I have fond memories of being able to ride around with him in the tractor, going to town, running errands, visiting with my grandfather, and doing other chores around the farm. These occasions were rare, and I would often be with his mother, my grandmother. She really was like another mother to me. My grandmother and I had the sweetest relationship, and she made me feel so special. She would take me everywhere with her, get me a treat or toy from the "dime store", and just talk and be with me. She taught me how to scan the ditches for baby's breath and make eggs. But my most favorite thing that she did for me was inviting all of my cousins over for a sleepover which only happened when I was in town. There were twenty-eight of us grandkids, not everyone made it, of course, but we would have so much fun. There was an undercurrent, a knowing by everyone, I was her favorite. Our time together was the best, and she made me feel so loved.

Unconditionally loved.

You see, my parents taught me so many amazing, poignant life skills, and I created very similar agreements with both of them, in order to protect my heart, the soft and tender spot we all have. The common thread with both of my parents was to be independently co-dependent, and as long as I played the role, I was loved.

Through my healing journey, I learned our parents have their own trauma, agreements, and issues, and they always did the best they could with what they had. I am forever grateful and love them dearly.

The unraveling and journey began when I experienced my first major loss.

It was 5:24 AM. I was twenty years old, living in Eugene, Oregon, thousands of miles away from anything that was familiar to me. The phone rang.

"Rach, it's your dad. Grandma passed away last night." I was receiving some of the worst news from my father.

"Keep it together Rach, calm, cool, collected," I thought.

"Ok, what are the plans?" I asked.

After explaining what he knew about the plans, he said, "We could fly you home for the funeral, but tickets will be about $1500." Not going has thus far been my only regret in life.

"Ok, let's talk later," I said as we hung up the phone.

On the way back to my room, my roommate asked, "What happened?"

 "My grandmother died," I responded

"What are you going to do?"

"Go back to bed."

As I lay there, memories swiped across the screen of my mind. I also, in those moments, understood all that was once familiar was about to change. I broke down and began to sob uncontrollably. I cried, curled up in a ball in the little room of my rental house. I was exhausted when all of a sudden, there was a sensation like someone had cocooned me in a weighted blanket full of calming, loving peace. I knew it was her, my grandmother. She was with me to soothe my grieving heart, and I drifted off to sleep.

Fast forward three years, I was twenty-three years old and engaged to my now-husband—the phone rings.

"Hey Rach, it's your mom. So I'm calling about your upcoming wedding. Do you think you could change the date? It conflicts with your sister's junior year homecoming, and since she is a cheerleader, she can't miss."

I hung up with disappointment hanging in my heart. I knew I would change the date, because how could my mom not be at my wedding? She was my best friend. My mom and I would talk at least five times a week, sometimes more. Something exciting or good would happen,

I'd call my mom. Something frustrating or bad would happen. I'd call my mom. If I was stuck and unsure what to do, I'd call my mom. She was my biggest supporter. Always. I could not imagine losing that, we changed the date and location of our wedding.

The phone rings.

"Hey, Rach, I got a joke for you."

"Ok, let's hear it."

Of course, I wanted to hear his joke, anything that would connect me to him. Even though I knew in my heart this joke was going to be sexist or racist, I'm going to have to laugh. I don't really think it's funny, but I laugh out loud and cry inside.

After I pretended I enjoyed his joke, the conversation would turn towards politics, family/town/friend gossip, or religion. Again, none of these topics interested me much, but I would listen and chime in just enough that it felt like I had his approval, and then we would hang up.

Later on, I found a connection piece with my father that I could get behind. He loved to offer his advice, and therefore, I often would check in with him to ensure my ideas and thoughts were "approved" by him before I made any major decisions. I felt it was important to do so because I had not been shown how to properly listen to and trust my own guidance system, my intuition. Remember that constant search for validation as a child? Here is how it showed up in my adult life, even when I was all grown-up and on my "own."

As you can see, up until this point, I failed to speak up, speak my mind, communicate properly, and set boundaries. There was so much fear around this—fear of losing what I cherished most in the world, my parents.

The unraveling continues.

"We are moving to Colorado!" I shared with so much excitement I could jump out of my skin. We had lived in Minnesota our whole marriage, twelve years at that point.

My father was so genuinely happy and supportive of this move. In fact, he was a big catalyst to making it happen.

My mother's response took me by surprise. Upon sharing this news with her, I heard a disappointment in her voice, and she asked, "What about me? When will I see my grandkids?"

We landed and settled in Colorado, a dream come true. For me personally, it was a twenty-year-old dream. I felt the shift. It wasn't a blatant in-your-face shift, simply an undercurrent flowing like that of a volcano ready to explode at any time.

We began adventuring immediately. It was why we had moved to CO, for the endless access of nature adventures. Our two boys, eight and four at the time, adapted quickly. We made it fun and created new experiences and memories. We all fell blissfully in love with our new home and the new routine of life. Every Sunday, I made it a point to call my mom. It was the only day of the week we were speaking. This went on for a few months, and then I got curious, "What if I didn't call?"

So I tested my curiosity and ceased my Sunday calls. Slowly I felt my heart begin to crack. For many weeks we did not speak. Then one day, my phone rang. It was my mother, and my heart lept with excitement.

"Hey Rach, calling to see if your sister and I could come out for a vacation." That was it, not to catch up, only to see if our house was open for them. My heart sank as I ended the call, and the crack began to deepen.

Deep in my knowing, this was the last time I would be with my mother for a long time. I arranged many adventures for us to do while they were visiting but not with the excitement one usually generates when planning for company.

The visit was fine, went fast, and was very surface level. When they left, I sat with how I was feeling. Something very unfamiliar to me. Up until that point, I wasn't one to tune into my feelings. Remember, it was an agreement that I made early on. Feelings were bad, to be ignored, pushed down, and most definitely not talked about. After really processing my emotions, I decided to write a letter to my mother and sister requesting time and space. This was my first big spoken boundary. It was scary as hell to mail those letters but, I did.

Deep down, I knew something in me needed to heal and heal in a way that did not allow for any wondering or questioning where I stood with them. I took control of the situation and my happiness and placed myself on the outside. It was a familiar strange sort of feeling being on the outside.

Since the big move, my relationship with my dad had gotten stronger, and once I created space with my mom, even more so. This was a dream of mine for so many years, to be close like this to him. We would talk multiple times a week, and I was an open book. We were sharing, asking for advice, and talking about nothing and everything. Having this dialogue with him made me feel so special and like I finally belonged in his world.

As the healing process began with my mother wound, feelings, thoughts, and lights of awareness shined onto my patterns and behaviors that no longer served me. Once the awareness is there, it is impossible to unsee.

Then one day, I realized, "Fuck, I carry the same patterns and behaviors with him too. Shit! I had dreamed of being in such a close relationship with him for so long, and now it is going to fall apart," were my thoughts.

Once this awareness came into view, the conversations with my father became hard work and challenging for me. I stopped asking his advice because I recognized I was only asking as a way to stay connected to him in some way. I began to use my voice more and more, which I knew made me vulnerable to losing his love. This created so much fear.

Fear of more loss.

Fear of losing the only parent I had left.

Fear of losing the rest of my siblings.

But above all else, fear of losing love.

My mantra became, "I just want it all to stop. I wish I could just hit the pause button." I was growing so tired and weary.

The phone rang.

"Rach I want to fly to see you and have breakfast, just you and I to sit and talk."

My first thought was, "Oh my god, he wants to take time to fly and see me." In practicing my new boundaries and finding my voice, I responded, with an empty kind of hope, "I would love to have breakfast with just you. As long as the conversation is about how we can move forward in our relationship."

His response crushed me and broke my heart into a million pieces.

"I'll send you a letter in June," he said.

While my heart crumbled to the earth below me, a sigh of relief washed over me. My days of acting were over. No more acting. No more agreements.

Here begins my dark night of the soul.

"Where do I even begin, and who am I?" I thought.

Little did I know, my journey had already begun, and all that was in store for me would bring me through to the light and love on the other side of this, discovering my bright, shining, loving soul.

I had been preparing for this exact moment my whole life. All of my experiences created a strength in me that I did not see until that point. I declared to create and design the life of my dreams.

All of the agreements I had made in the past were now gone—what a dizzying feeling. The deep grooves of those belief systems were so deeply ingrained in my mind, thus the biggest challenge of all was right in front of me, myself.

"Where do I even begin, and who am I?" I asked again.

I began working with a therapist who had a very unique approach, yet somewhat traditional. She helped me through a number of rough days and weeks. However, I didn't feel this was the answer.

I tried something new. I planted myself across from an intuitive, recommended to me by a dear and trusted friend.

"Welcome, Rachel. What brings you in today?"

"Nothing specifically, I'm doing pretty good. Just see what comes up maybe?"

"Ok, which parent would you like to talk about first?"

Well shit, she nailed it. This started my healing on a deep energetic level. It was how I began to see all of my actions, from the lens of energetic vibration. I had many sessions with Francesca, this intuitive, and I just loved being in her presence. So much healing occurred in that space; it was beautiful.

In March of 2020, I was very strongly guided to take her course called "The Power of Tribe: A Spiritual Commitment to Self." It was here, I started to see the Light and began moving out of this dark night of the soul.

In this in-person class, Francesca took us through intentional practices that assisted us in healing our trauma on a generational level. With the foundation of the class designed to assist in healing the mother and father wounds, true healing occurred.

In one of the exercises, while in meditation, we were to feel unconditional love come from our mother's side to our navel center. I felt such a thick and powerful energetic exchange of love during this time. It was absolutely incredible. I could feel the love my mother had and continues to have for me.

We were then guided to repeat this on our father's side to our navel. The expectations had been set, so when what happened next left me feeling so confused. As we were asked to feel the unconditional love flowing between the two of us, my throat began to tighten and constrict. I was struggling to breathe. I tried to connect with my breath, working to take a deep inhale that was stopped with each effort. I sat through the rest of the exercise, searching frantically to feel the love come in, and as she guided us back to the room, I screamed, "NO! NO! NO! NO!" in my mind. "I hadn't felt his love yet."

For the duration of the class, I sat so confused, in and out of taking in new content, while asking, "What the fuck was that?"

As the class came to a close, many participants were asking questions, one of which led to a demonstration with two random people in the group. As Francesca was answering the question using these two people, she made a sound that resonated so profoundly in my core, and I began to sob. As she stood at the front of the class, mid-sentence, sobbing, I knew I was connected to this moment and her experience somehow. I felt it in all of my being. I said in my head, "Yes, that is how I felt. This is for me." I didn't know "what" was for me, but something with her in that moment was connected to my path.

At the end of class, I was returning some of her things to the front table. As I approached the front, she caught me and said, "Oh Rachel." gave me the biggest hug and said, "That power that came through, that was for you."

"I know, I felt it," I said.

I quickly rushed out of the room and to my truck, where I wept tears that had waited years to be released. On that first day of March 2020, I had stepped into my knowledge and power of living my rich, authentically aligned, wholesome life.

"So, what do I do now?" I wondered.

It was a remembering. All of the stories, experiences, and tools I had been collecting on my journey came flooding into plain sight, and it was time to begin.

I began putting the tools to use by connecting my body, mind, and spirit.

It started with food. Having the awareness and being able to witness the energetic vibration of food, I dialed in my eating habits even further. Those that know me best know I love to talk, prepare, and be around food. Not just any kind of food, real, raw food—food that is brought to us from Mother Earth herself. With each passing day of eating in a way that brought positive, energetic nourishment into my life, I began to "see" more. This inadvertently balanced my microbiome, which had, once again, become unbalanced.

Along with providing myself with nutritious energy, I was moving my body. I LOVE movement. I mean, I was a physical education teacher for over fifteen years. Hikes, walks, strength-building, yoga, and more yoga were part of my daily routine. Moving my body makes me feel my best, allows me to tune into and feel, feel where I am holding tension, and most importantly, feel my own strength.

My meditation had been a non-negotiable for over a year, however, it began to expand, and I was watching my ability to co-create with the Universe, with God. Watching my desires and dreams begin to unfold in real-time. My meditation practice also allowed me to become aware of when I would get off track, where old habits wanted to creep back in and gave me the ability to stay committed to myself.

We are human, having a human experience. I had moments, and still do, of weakness. It is in those moments that I call upon my own personal mantra. This mantra is one of my creations. It offers me the strength to continue to put one foot in front of the other. A reminder of the brightness of my light and to let it shine.

As I connected deeper with my soul, my guides moved me closer to my mission, my purpose, and my Dharma. I, like many of you, hold a strong desire to help others. I realized I had been planning and preparing for this my whole life. It was my time. I was being lovingly pushed to my service in the world. Thus the Live Your RAW Life platform and podcast were birthed. All of this knowledge I had gained through healing myself was to be shared with the world, for you and the world to heal.

The healing is easy; the commitment and consistency is the hard part. This is why I created the Restoring Harmony program. This 12-week private immersion gives participants accountability, guideposts, and loving support along the way to their own ascension. This is a road untraveled by you, and past programming, thoughts, behaviors, and patterns could keep you stuck or, worse, sliding backward. Having a guide to walk alongside you offers the support to get to the root of where you are holding yourself back in living a life full of peace, love, and joy.

These agreements that I made with my parents throughout my lifetime allowed for a certain level of control in my world that was full of the unexpected. They protected me, my heart. They offered a sanctuary where everything in my life felt uneasy. They served their purpose. I am forever grateful, and it was with this gratitude that I released the agreements forever.

I hold even more gratitude for my healing journey. Many walked the path with me, and I am fortunate and blessed. The strength and ability to step into my power, own it, and use it to assist many others on their own journey is beyond what I could ever have imagined I would have the honor of doing in this lifetime—what a gift.

If you know your body, mind, and spirit are out of alignment, now is the time to begin. Restore harmony within your microbiome, move your body, practice mindfulness, root into meditation, create your personal mantra, and discover your mission. That is "Restoring Harmony."

My wish for you, dear friend, is for you too to feel freedom from the agreements you have unknowingly made. That your internal guidance system moves you into inspired action. Action to take YOUR power back, heal from within, and let your gifts shine in the world. When you are ready to begin, I will be here holding the light.

ABOUT THE AUTHOR

RACHEL ANNE WATKINS

Public school teacher turned intuitive and holistic health guide Rachel Anne Watkins has not only positively shifted the trajectory of her life but her client's lives as well. Rachel received her Bachelor of Science degree in Health and Physical Education in 2005. She used that to teach in public schools for over 15 years. Recently she graduated from the Institute of Integrative Nutrition out of New York City, which granted her her health coaching certificate.

Rachel lives in the Rocky Mountains with her husband, their two boys, and an ever-loyal Australian Shepard.

Rachel uses the knowledge and experiences gained over the past decade to help her clients remove stress, anxiety, and overwhelm through developing consistent habits and behaviors that restore health and harmony within their bodies, mind, and spirit in order for them to discover their mission in life. Her very unique and all-encompassing modality and process align clients to live their rich, authentically aligned, wholesome lives.

To connect further with Rachel and enhance your healing journey, you can find your next steps at:

Website: www.liveyourrawlife.com

Email: raw@liveyourrawlife.com

Instagram: www.instagram.com/liveyourrawlife/

Facebook: www.facebook.com/liveyourrawlife

TINA SIMONE MOWATT REECE

HEAL YOUR WOMB & BECOME A PORTAL OF LIFE

INTRODUCTION:

For many women, becoming pregnant and giving birth is wishful thinking. Many of us have tried unsuccessfully to become pregnant and give birth to a child or children, and we question our worthiness of the happy family life we envision. I have been there, and I know the anguish, fears, and physical suffering you have endured to try to make motherhood a reality. After numerous surgeries and years upon years of pain and suffering, I too unconsciously assimilated limiting beliefs, questioning my sanity at times when I swore I could feel a baby moving in my womb. I hope my story will inspire, encourage and comfort you, and most importantly, help you realize - you, dear one, are a Mother, a Portal of Life. The names of persons I refer to in my story have been changed to protect their identity.

Tina Simone Mowatt Reece
Founder: Xayla Trinity Empowerment Services
Life Coach- Empowerment & Life Purpose Author, Speaker

HEAL YOUR WOMB & BECOME A PORTAL OF LIFE

I sat in my car one evening, drunk with the sugar high I treated myself to—ice cream is a super delicious distraction from the monotony and stress of everyday living. It was also time for me to escape for a moment and breathe.

I slipped into what I would call *Nothing Land* - It felt like the place we go before waking or falling into a deep sleep. I did not plan on doing this, not in public with my car windows down, but I drifted into *Nothing Land...*

"Mummy! I am here! Hurry up and find Father so I can come!"

I felt a cool breeze gently stroking my left cheek when I leaned against the car door. I was almost sure I heard a high-pitched voice whispering those words to me. Even if I wanted to, this euphoric place compelled me to stay—it was such a happy place where I felt inner peace and comfort.

I was jolted out of my stupor when one of the patrons of this famous ice-cream sweet spot in Kingston, Jamaica, became very impatient with the security guard taking his time to lift the barrier so he could leave the premises. I checked the clock on my dashboard and realized I was in my happy place, *Nothing Land*, for a little over half an hour! Did that just happen? I questioned myself half-heartedly because while my brain could not compute those thirty-plus minutes, my heart was dancing for joy.

The dreams I related to home and family began forming at age nine —my mother told me one fateful, explosive evening, she and my father were ending their marriage. The news brought a mixture of relief and sadness, and I came to terms with the emerging realities. I decided then and there my future family life would be very different from what I had experienced. In addition to the loving and kind husband who would be with me forever, I saw visions of a sprawling one-story home, white picket fence, green grass, and flowers all around. I would have at least two dogs—one toy breed and another fierce and trained guard dog. I visualized a blissful euphoria and two beautiful children—the firstborn would be a beautiful girl who would look like me, and her name would begin with A—I had no idea why it had to be an A. Then, my second-born, a handsome, mischievous, and energetic boy who would look like his father, dimples in cheeks et al. I imprinted the vision in my mind, and it became more defined and multidimensional with each new life experience. The picture of my perfect family life took on some inexplicable hues, and I became more focused on what having a child meant to me.

One evening in my pre-teen years, I heard a commotion outside on the street. An adult male voice was cursing and shouting, and a childlike voice wailed in agony. My stomach churned as I lept towards the window to peer at what was going on. I wish I did not look. No sooner than I moved the curtains, I saw a man holding a boy by his collar and using his other fisted hand to punch the boy's small frame in his abdomen over and over again. I felt every punch and hurriedly moved away from the window, feeling each traumatic blow myself. I trembled and rushed to the phone to call the police—thank goodness the police station was only a block away. I dialed, thinking at the same time what I was going to say. My hands froze—simultaneously, I relived my father's raised, belted hand coming to lash my younger body. I froze when I was about to call the police to save the child. This terrible scene was too much to handle, and I decided on a different course of action. I quietly replaced the phone on the receiver and consoled myself that an adult would help him better than I ever could. I painted some dark shadows in the picture of my perfect family life and clutched my womb. My family life would never involve violent experiences, I resolved with myself—physically striking a child as punishment for mistakes was out of the question!

My passion for the rights of children was born after the terrible incident. I filed it away, like I did other horrific experiences, and went on with my chatter-filled, extroverted, happy child persona. Despite the broken parental relationship, my close-knit extended maternal relatives provide a cushion and safety net I needed to continue to flourish.

Puberty was tumultuous! I, the effervescent, talkative tomboy who was in no rush to grow older! I had my cohort of friends, mainly boys —girls were a bit too complicated. The inevitable came and with it excruciating physical pain and anguish. Why me? My mother and older sister did not experience the wide variety of debilitating symptoms I did during menstruation, and they were unable to empathize with my monthly ordeal. I felt very alone and angered by physical puberty! Why is my body fighting me? Dysmenorrhea, backaches, vomiting, clots, and depression became a monthly experience and I tried my best to cope with little emotional support. I thought the nurse at school would understand, but to her, I was an unnecessary distraction from her daily phone calls to her friends gossiping about the private lives of the girls at my high school. I was unaccustomed to being sick, but at age 19, I started my journey of being what I called a *professional patient*. It was also the age I began my romantic relationship journey. Darrell was cute, shy, very conservative with his words, and almost clumsy with his emotional expressions. He was my boy-next-door sweetheart and the person who took me to my first gynecological visit. I thought having a female doctor was a wise choice because she would understand what I was going through. When we arrived at the doctor's office, we were both nervous but determined to find out what was causing the ever-increasing monthly discomforts. The doctor scornfully rejected my claims of being a virgin while I lay naked and exposed, both physically and emotionally.

"But you have stretch marks! You look like you have been pregnant before!"

This female doctor had not even begun to examine me before she cast her judgments. I had recently recovered from an acute throat infection and had lost considerable weight in a short period. I stormed out of the doctor's office, swearing I would NEVER go to another female gynecologist EVER AGAIN! Poor Darrell was at a loss for words and tried unsuccessfully to console me. What was ironic about the experience and having stretch marks was Darrell ending our relationship a few years later because I was too overweight. He had the home, the white picket fence, and he loved dogs. I thought he would have been my dream husband.

SCARS & TEARS

A few years after my fateful first gynecological visit, I received the dreaded endometriosis diagnosis. Dr. Guthrie, my new gynecologist, delivered the diagnosis, along with diagrams and charts to clearly explain what was possibly happening in my womb. Alas, the only way to have a confirmed diagnosis was to go under the knife! A previous doctor had toyed with the idea I had the disease, but he shrugged it off, declaring I was too young for endometriosis to be a correct diagnosis. By then, I was learning to trust my intuition more and more as my faith in the medical fraternity was continually eroded each time I encountered a clueless doctor. I could only depend on myself in the final analysis.

As I scheduled my first surgery, I looked at my family life dream that was now constantly in the forefront of my mind. My relationship with Darrell came crashing because I was not good enough, and now my body seemed not good enough either. The colors, hues, vitality, and ethereal quality of my dream began to fade, and with it, my longing to be a wife and mother. Why was my womb failing me??

One year later, I had a new beau, a healing body, and an exciting job. I obsessively researched endometriosis, infertility, and alternative healing modalities. One year later, I received a diagnosis of a large fibroid. Surgery became necessary based on the size and position of the fibroid, and my despair increased. It was the best and worst time of my life, and though I was prepared mentally and financially for this more invasive surgery, I became emotionally disconnected from my womb. My womb was morphing into a monster and now challenged my life. My beau, who later became my fiancé, resembled the perfect support system I needed. Ryan was tall, muscular, mysterious, and as emotionally detached as I was to my womb. I had a type!

I awoke from the second surgery and was shocked by unexpected news. In addition to removing the endometrial deposits causing my distress, my right ovary was excised. I secretly wondered then and years later if there was a sinister plan to sabotage my family life dreams. Ryan was supportive throughout the ordeal, and like Darrell, our relationship ended a few years after the surgery. Thirteen years later, however, I heard from his good friend that his alleged reason for departing was because he was afraid I could not have a child. He moved on quickly after our breakup and married a much younger woman who was, I heard, pregnant during their wedding ceremony.

Endometriosis manifested yet again six years after my second surgery —this time a six-year reprieve. Surgery was scheduled for the third time, and I found myself consoling my in-hospital roommate the night before our respective myomectomies, sharing with her what she could expect and encouraging her to have a positive mindset beforehand.

My consultant did not have good news for me during our post-surgery review a week later:

"If this recurs, I will have no other choice but to recommend a full hysterectomy. The only way to become pregnant is through IVF. It is an expensive process with little guarantee of success, especially with your medical history."

I walked out of his office that day after hearing those words and never returned. I needed to be healed, body, mind, and spirit! My childhood dream of a happy family life faded, and I dumped it in the shadows of my unconscious mind.

"Why am I not enough?"

"Don't I deserve happiness?"

"Why can't my dreams come true?"

"I can't bear this any longer."

Words from friends and loved ones, mostly intending to help but some unsolicited, served only to add to my pain, anger, and hopelessness:

"Having a child isn't everything you know."

"You don't need to give birth to a child to be a mother."

"Karma is a bitch."

I began to move away from my traditional life in search of healing. I became a brooding, intense woman who decided that what was needed was a more realistic vision of the future. Religion, conventional medicine, and even some friendships became collateral damage. I needed answers. I needed to fully understand my body and reestablish emotional connection instead of embracing the self-hatred threatening to overtake me. This was a solo journey, and the prescribed roles of wife, mother, corporate professional, academic genius, and friend-extraordinaire held no appeal nor the answers to my inner quest. I increasingly withdrew into myself, and the ensuing crisis had me questioning my sanity.

DARK NIGHT OF THE SOUL

Some call this place purgatory, where nothing made sense, the relevant now irrelevant, and the way forward was a dark cloudy highway to certain hell. To add to the fright of this limbo, I also stumbled into my psychic and clairvoyant gifts.

"How did I know the woman was pregnant?"

"How can I feel the emotions of friends and even strangers?"

"Why do I keep having these vague illnesses?"

"Is that man going to die from a clogged colon?"

"WHO THE HELL AM I?"

I began to have memories, impossible memories of lives before. Yes, I do mean past lives. My once superficial interest in astrology over the years became a full-blown pursuit as it seemed to hold keys to my self-discovery. Answers to my questions began to flow to me from taboo places, and my mother warned me anxiously about venturing there. In her experience, she witnessed my father's sojourn of a similar nature, and as far as she perceived it, his inevitable destruction came from such explorations. I heeded to an extent because I saw firsthand how easy it became for others to choose a shadowy and power-hungry existence. I trusted my heart and mind and knew I had no interest or yearning for such experiences. The occult world is exactly what it means, a *hidden world*, and we are programmed to fear the unseen. My journey to self took me along hidden, occult paths. I was afraid, but the strong knowing I was being *divinely guided* overrode my fears. My mother and a few close friends became worried I had veered from the prescribed paths, but others appeared in my life along the way, and their empowering assistance helped me along the way. I eventually recognized my hidden purpose: seeking answers to the baffling experiences of my life inspired me to help others with their journeys.

HEALING BEGINS

For a few years, I immersed myself into a space where I explored alternative healing modalities such as Homeopathy, Acupuncture, Reiki, EFT Tapping, and most recently, Applied Kinesiology. Through these modalities, in addition to various forms of divination from multiple schools of philosophy and cultures, I slowly but surely began forming a new relationship with my beautiful body. Indeed! I'm overweight, as my first love pointed out. I had not conceived a child, as my ex-fiancé secretly shared with others, but I began to love my body unconditionally. I came into the consciousness of how my body allows me to have a physical experience. My body has such profound innate wisdom! It is designed to preserve my life at all costs and allow a sensory experience as a spirit having an earthly journey. My past experiences began to hold deep meaning for me, even the unpleasant ones. I slowly aligned with a yearning to serve humanity - to protect the child who endured punches in his stomach, becoming the listening ear to those who needed empathy and consolation, providing insights when asked, and sharing my inner feminine beauty. I began to paint a picture of me, Tina, transforming and becoming Xayla. The name Xayla came to me one day while meditating and connecting with God. I often would get a pen and write, letting each word flow one after the other without forethought. The words would flow as they do now, and it would be sometime later when I fully understood the meaning and depth of the words I channeled. Xayla is a personification of my re-empowered self, and it is now a part of the name of my organization officially formed in 2020 - *Xayla Trinity Empowerment Services.*

My continued healing and re-discovery of myself created room for my initial childhood dreams to re-emerge. I met my beloved husband over six years ago, and we inexplicably recognized each other immediately. His name, Kyril, means *Lord,* and I jokingly told him I would NEVER call him Lord! Before we met, I had already shelved the idea of finding my initial dream husband and satisfied myself with connecting with the best man for me - the apparition I would conjure during my nightly meditations. I imagined my love sitting across from me and join me in my nightly ritual. I saw his face then, smiling and comforting, and I was no longer alone. My meditation mate was enough—I needed to focus on my healing and helping others.

"Kyril is too good to be true."

I still had some unhealed spaces inside my heart, and I unconsciously told myself he was going to disappoint me like others before. I ran from Kyril, my beloved, for about five weeks, feeding him some inadequate reason for running away. I was getting too close and was uncomfortable with being vulnerable, receptive, and trusting. In essence, I was uncomfortable with my feminine energies. Why couldn't I have my meditative mate who would come to me at my will, smile, and comfort me? My inner guidance system had other ideas and nagged me until I phoned him one life-changing Friday, May 13th. It was one of the best decisions I have made in my life, and we have been inseparable ever since! He introduced me to his world and his little golden child, Adrianna. He allowed us to find our way to each other, and slowly but surely, his little girl became our little girl.

We got married after living together for almost three years, and life settled down and blossomed for me, for us. I began to play more with the idea of having my own company, picturing a healing center, offering alternative physical healing modalities, life coaching, and counseling services. Can this be true! I went scurrying into the dark recesses of my pain of long ago to find the picture of my childhood dream—a husband, children, two dogs, a large one-story home complete with a white picket fence. My picture was crumpled but still present, and I blended it with my new vision of healing and service. Oh my goodness! This picture was much more glorious than I had first conceived! I finally found the happiness I thought I did not deserve. I soon discovered that healing is a continuous journey, and the more we evolve and heal, the more unhealed spaces in our unconscious mind would re-emerge, sometimes quite dramatically.

I got a pale-positive pregnancy test!

My body was feeling weird for a few weeks. Despite several ailments and scars in my womb and reproductive system, my menstrual cycle continued like clockwork. I ignored the fact my period was a few days late—perhaps this is to be expected at forty-something years old. Adrianna, however, insisted on something brewing. She started to poke my belly while giggling and pointing to the television each time a baby appeared. I secretly purchased two pregnancy tests and checked.

My heart pounded as I waited for what I felt would be inevitable—one line only. My husband and I spoke about children before we got married, and I told him it was not likely to happen. We were happy caring for Adrianna as our only child - if we wanted another child later, we would adopt. The day I saw a faint second line appearing after 3 minutes, I slipped immediately into *Nothing Land*.

I knew this feeling. The cool brush of wind on my cheeks and a high-pitched distant whisper drifted into my meditative space for what seemed like a few seconds. With my third eye now wide open, I saw my child. I held my breath, unable to process a coherent thought as I frantically showed the barely visible second line on the pregnancy test to my husband. I was elated and terrified while he struggled to see the affirming line. Was I pregnant?? Can this be happening? All the suppressed fears, anguish, and trauma pushed to the surface of my consciousness. I was a mess!

Pseudocyesis—I received this terrible diagnosis when we finally ventured to the doctor to confirm pregnancy. I did not dare take another test because I was terrified the faint line would disappear. I convinced the doctor to perform an ultrasound, and confirmation of pseudocyesis, phantom pregnancy, was cemented as we looked at the image of an empty womb. Was I not healed? Did I not do all I needed to do to heal, come to terms with reality and even move forward with supporting others on their journey? *What is this phantom pregnancy crap?*

History seemed to have repeated itself. I was happy, and now the rug had been pulled from under me. My newly created picture of forever happiness began to take on shadowy hues of grey like once before. If you can believe it, I had this rare diagnosis two more times over the next three years. I struggled terribly with the experience, and predictably, it negatively impacted my relationship with my loved ones at home. How tragic! Right?

Wrong. My inner guidance system was not so gently reminding me I had an unhealed space left inside needing closure and the creation of a new story.

This deeply buried space was about my son from a past lifetime. The beckoning I heard quietly in my mind at the ice cream locale, and each time I looked at a pale positive pregnancy test was the memory of him. He was an echo of an unhealed wound I had been carrying for much too long—it was time to let go. The manifestation of disease, trauma, and anguish in this current life journey mirrored the sorrows of long ago. It was only then I realized that the people who came in and out of my life all played a significant role in my womb healing journey. The insensitive female doctor, the gentle Dr. Guthrie, the breakup of my parents, the child being punched, my failed relationships, and even the wicked pseudocyesis diagnosis were people and experiences helping me recognize the source of my pain and to finally heal. My long-lost son needed to heal as well and be set free. He was caught in-between worlds, feeling responsible for my pain and obligated to incarnate through my body to make me happy.

WOUNDS TO WISDOM

Healing my womb went way beyond the physical realms for me, and I made the journey for my sake and the sake of my loved ones. My husband stood by me as we symbolically released my son, our son, and called my womb into wholeness. I am no longer burdened by echoes of the past, and the memory of my son is finally liberated. I now recall my divine authority to choose whether or not I truly want to conceive and give birth to a child.

Women have been disempowered for centuries, led to believe conceiving a child is beyond our choosing and determined totally by external factors. Conceiving a child and pregnancy should be a manifestation of a woman's conscious and pure agreement to allow the incarnation of a soul through her body. An empowered woman deciding on pregnancy is not consumed by a need to satiate pain and anguish, nor anxieties to satisfy cultural, gender, and familial expectations. The root word of conception, conceive, is a mental process and therefore internal. I know now from my healing journey that I was filled with pain and guilt, and consequently, my reality followed suit. Conscious manifestation is a more involved process, and it does not mean mere thinking will guarantee manifestation. Similarly, our unwanted experiences are not merely a result of unconscious, negative thoughts, though they are involved.

Being a Portal of Life includes but is not restricted to pregnancy and giving birth to a child. Becoming a Portal of Life is facilitating the manifestation of tangible creations. Whatever we birth, create, and manifest is our offspring. We tap into our co-creative powers and begin the awesome creative journey. Think about it! Everything you see around you, a pencil, cell phone, this book, was conceived with human thought! We as a human collective have endured centuries of disempowering consciousness programming, disconnecting us from our authority to choose and co-create under Divine Direction. Becoming a Portal of Life involves the feminine attributes of introspection, meditation, reflection, nurture, wisdom, and even compassion, combined with the masculine attributes of reason, action, logic, drive, discipline, and confidence.

I have co-created what I call a journey—an empowerment course offered by *Xayla Trinity Empowerment Services*, the first of many to come. This course, *i-SUPERNOVA*, helps participants realign with their authentic selves and live life from a centered place. Alignment with our authentic self is an important ingredient to enjoying a happy life, not freed from challenges but empowered to overcome and learn from all our experiences. The journey also includes initiating the process of comprehending and healing relationships, appreciating every person as soulmates helping us evolve, whether the relationship is smooth and beautiful or dreadfully difficult. We believe our empowerment course sets all participants on the track to consciously make authentic choices and co-create whatever they want to manifest. *i-SUPERNOVA* reflects my journey and is one of the many *babies* I chose to give birth to before leaving this lifetime. The upcoming course offering to be launched in 2022—closely named after this chapter, is designed to help women who want to become mothers choose this path from a space of authenticity, empowerment, and happiness. I want to remind you, beautiful women reading these words, that conceiving a child and choosing to be a Portal of Life is a divine authority you possess, and the only significant validation and empowerment you need lie within you.

My true dream of becoming a mother manifested long before I grasped it and has now transformed into the much bigger picture of my purpose - helping you on your journey. I smile now, typing these last words with one hand while my other hand lies gently on my womb.

ABOUT THE AUTHOR

TINA SIMONE REECE

Tina Simone Reece is a Jamaican woman dedicated to offering her many gifts and talents to helping others live an authentic and empowered life. Her current mission and purpose have been influenced by nearly 30 years of work experience, serving others in multiple industries and roles in the fields of client services, business operations, and business administration. She is also a psychic intuitive, astrologer, and a certified life purpose life coach and applies the multiple dimensions of herself to all of her endeavors.

In 2020, Tina unveiled her current passion as Founder and Life Purpose & Empowerment Coach of *Xayla Trinity Empowerment Services*. With her recently completed Life Coaching Certification, Tina has been actively fine-tuning the coaching programs and servicing clients internationally. She is planning an official launch of her website in 2022, which will include other writing works, music, and weekly video programs. Her second course, also to be launched in 2022, will serve women who want to authentically align with motherhood and journey through woundedness into empowerment.

As a wife, mother, and entrepreneur, Tina feels that sharing herself with her loved ones and the world, using her many gifts, is the key to living a happy, authentic and inspiring life.

Connect with Tina
Facebook: https://m.facebook.com/104004424549187/
Instagram: www.instagram.com/xayla.trinity/

VALERIE SMITH

YOUR CIRCUMSTANCES DON'T DEFINE YOU: A JOURNEY OF TRANSFORMATION AND HEALING

INTRODUCTION:

*T*he words on the pages that follow are simply that, words —the gift of a journey.

Trauma really does confront you with the best and the worst. You see the horrendous things that people do to each other, but you also see resiliency, the power of love, the power of caring, the power of commitment to oneself, the knowledge that there are things that are larger than our individual survival. And in some ways, I don't think you can appreciate the glory of life unless you also know the dark side of life.

- *Bessel Van Der Kolk, MD*

Writing this chapter has been quite cathartic. A permission of sorts to find my voice, my self-expression. If you feel a sense of relatedness in the words that I share, I'm sorry. Know you are not alone. May you feel heard. May you give yourself permission to dream, to heal, and to thrive.

In our culture, we associate vulnerability with emotions we want to avoid, such as fear, shame, and uncertainty. Yet, we too often lose sight of the fact that vulnerability is also the birthplace of joy, belonging, creativity, authenticity, and love.

- Brene Brown

Valerie Smith
Integrative Healer, and lifelong learner

YOUR CIRCUMSTANCES DON'T DEFINE YOU: A JOURNEY OF TRANSFORMATION AND HEALING

We were raised to be independent beings from the time we could walk, so it made sense that I chose to leave home at 13. I couldn't bear to be beaten one more time. As a police officer paid a visit to the house that evening, I was quite clear. The only way to get me to stay was to handcuff me to my bed. Earlier that day was the last time he would ever hurt me. He found me in my room, ripped the rotary phone out of the socket, pushed me into the wall as he beat the phone into my body. I braced my head, was quiet, and stayed as still as I could. It would pass. It always does. When his rage ended, he ordered me outside to chop wood. As soon as I was out of the house, I ran five blocks to where my sister was staying. She had left six months prior after the worst beating of them all. She had half her hair pulled out of her head and bruises all over her body. I remember these days vividly. Me trying to get him off of them. Running to call 911 and in those moments felt like I failed, like I couldn't protect them. Like it was my fault. He was a sick fuck. Literally. We later found letters and pictures he wrote confessing to the beatings he gave women and how bad he hurt them. Somehow we found ways to laugh about it.

Growing up with the notion that children were better seen than heard, where we didn't speak about our emotions, express ourselves or have a difference of opinion. If I did, there were consequences. Fuck, if I didn't, there were consequences. Anything could happen at any time.

I was a tough kid, like a rock. I was closed off. Actually, I was numb. Trapped in the illusion that nothing bothered me. I stopped feeling the feelings. Gone were the days that I would be in class, sitting at my desk, hiding the bruises on my body, hiding the hurt in my heart, while a tear rolled down my cheek. Feeling alone, I managed to always have a smile on my face. I went on with life, that's how we managed it. The bullshit was water off my back. Even when I learned of other kids who moved into my house, sure, it was temporary, but nothing felt good about knowing another kid was living in my room, riding my bike.

I was smoking, drinking, and getting high, and sometimes hanging with the wrong crowd. I was going to the wrong parties. Like the one in that basement where my drink was spiked, and I was gang-raped— waking up at a friend's house the next day, not knowing how I got there. She tossed me my underwear and said, "girl, you were raped last night." I left with so much shame. Shame that I would carry around for decades. My inner critic: how could I be so stupid? I should have known better. I never spoke of it again and buried it deep.

School was hard. I couldn't focus. I dropped out after a half-assed grade 10. I worked a lot, often multiple jobs. I intended to do what I could to keep my sister in school.

At 17, I stopped doing drugs. Most of my friends were just beginning, and I was done. I couldn't take the paranoia. I had this idea that I could sense what people were feeling and thinking, which freaked me out.

I had no words to describe the panic attacks I hid from the world. Keeping it all in, at times, I felt crazy or like I was going to die. My coping mechanism became water. As long as I could take a sip of water, I knew that I was still alive. This went on for years.

People have a range of capacities to deal with overwhelming experience. Some people, some kids particularly, are able to disappear into a fantasy world, to dissociate, to pretend like it isn't happening, and are able to go on with their lives. And sometimes it comes back to haunt them.

- Bessel Van Der Kolk, MD

When I was hired on at the bank, I didn't expect to stay there for 18 years. I remember meeting employees in various departments who had been there 10, 15, 20+ years and thinking (as if facing a life sentence), not me, no way. I'm here now, but I'll be out of here soon. After returning from a sabbatical, I created the motto that each year I was either going to learn more or earn more. This served me well. I climbed the corporate ladder and was involved in really great projects, held amazing jobs, and worked with incredible people. I found my skill set, what I was good at. I had a knack for connecting with others, learning processes in any department, and proposing and implementing change that would create efficiency, reduce risk, and improve morale. My gift—connecting the dots. I asked hard questions, built relationships, and wasn't afraid to challenge the status quo or the mindset "it's been this way forever." In parallel, I lived in fear. Fear that I would get caught. With every promotion, especially when I worked in Audit and Governance and when I became a Director of Finance. I was scared that somehow they would find out the truth. Twelve years into my career, behind the scenes, at 34, through correspondence, I had officially graduated high school and earned my Ontario Secondary School Diploma. It was important to me that I completed this. This was my way of making it right. Plus, I had this idea that if I ever had kids, I wanted this to be an example to them.

For a long time, I wanted to meet someone, have a real relationship, and to connect. I had experiences here and there. Most fizzled out when the physical attraction wore off. Rooted in sex, any sign of depth was a signal to leave. Except for this special one. I didn't know the love I felt until I lost it. It snuck up on me. Not what I was expecting. The greatest of friendship mixed in with a twist of excitement. Two things got in the way: the shame and embarrassment of being with a woman and my fixation on the idea that I would meet someone else whom I was truly holding out for, a man. She grew tired of this story and eventually went about her way. My heart was broken. I vowed within myself that it was better to live and love than to never experience love at all.

Returning from my sabbatical, I joined the boys (and a few gals) for the usual Friday night shinny. My yearlong adventure overseas was amazing. A big insight I came home with was—in order to love, I would have to accept someone for who they are, for their strengths, and opportunities for improvement. That last sentence hits me hard as I type this (I'm still learning this one). That Friday night, I met the man that I would eventually marry.

Our relationship progressed quickly. We were living together within a few months and buying our first property within the year. Five years in, standing in the bedroom of our second home, I shocked myself with my own words, "I know I never wanted to get married nor have kids, but I think I am meant to procreate, and I want to have your children."

The idea of kids is one thing; actually being responsible for them is another. After my daughter was born, the anxiety came back. I was in over my head and had no clue what I was doing. Wishing someone would share the manual with me. Not knowing how to manage or understand my emotions, let alone those of another human who doesn't have words. I was overwhelmed. My deepest fear kicked in, and I didn't want to repeat what I grew up with.

We reconnected after 20 years. We caught up on the adventures of life and the pressing news that my mom was in the hospital, and the odds were not good. She asked, "why do you think that is?" My reply "likely because my mom doesn't deal with things." The irony hits me. A shameful secret that plagues me each day, one I thought I would take to my death bed, was actually going to make me sick. That night during my RCIA class, we were doing the stations of the cross. I deeply felt the message of Jesus' life. His acceptance of others and standing in his truths. Tears roll down my eyes. I must tell him.

As long as you keep secrets and suppress information, you are fundamentally at war with yourself. - Bessel Van Der Kolk, MD

"There's something I need to tell you." Scared AF, embarrassed, and ashamed, I begin. "Remember when I said I wasn't happy and wanted our marriage to end. I was having an affair. I'm sorry." For the next few weeks, there was a lot of upset, a lot of pain. I felt terrible. I was hurting him all over again. I still cry at this truth—the selfishness—to act and follow that curiosity and then the need to confess. The underlying truth, we weren't happy, and we didn't really know it, nor have the skills or the examples to get through it. For a long while, we connected more deeply and made love more passionately than ever.

Over the years, I changed, and we grew apart as a result. The things we once connected on, we didn't anymore. Underlying, I had this idea that I wanted him to change with me. I thought I was encouraging, but I've come to realize I wasn't supportive. I wanted something for him other than he wanted for himself. The irony of my realization that led me to him.

I never thought the day would come. It rocked me. Energetically making sense, but feeling the hurt and rejection as abandonment was familiar. We had grown apart. We were living together, raising kids, career-focused and disconnected. He declared it: he wasn't happy, and in summary, there was nothing we could do. We both felt the truth in that. I felt like I failed.

It's like I hit rock bottom: Leaving my career of 18 years, I left a community, a place I 'grew up' in, daily routines, connections, built-in discipline, a sense of confidence in the work I knew I could do, and the idea of safety in the biweekly paycheck. My marriage ended, and so did our 15-year relationship. I had a side hustle that I wasn't performing in. I lost a close friend. And I was now faced with the greatest challenge: to be alone with my kids. Fear that I would repeat my familiar past, that I would get angry and explosive at them, that it would develop into an uncontrollable rage.

As I look back on the 3.5 years since we split, I am filled with so much love and gratitude for the mother and person I have become and the connection I have with my kids. I am so frickin proud of myself. I took that fear and my self-doubt, and I made it my biggest mission— to be an incredible mom to my kids and to my own inner child. I weep. Tears strolled down my eyes. If I got one thing right, it's in how I love and am present for my kids and my commitment to keep doing that. I don't have it perfect, but I have a ton of compassion for them and for me. We are good. We are safe. We are loved. We are connected. They will likely still need tons of therapy when they grow up, but I think we all do. I am trusting that we each have our own journey, which means they have theirs.

. . .

My journey of transformation has been no small feat. I believe deeply that I am healing generational wounds and changing the trajectory for myself, my kids, and the generations to come.

For years I have had the self-narrative: I am broken pieces, a fraud, and better off on my own. People leave. And that I am sick and am going to die. Yes, eventually, but not yet.

Through the trials and tribulations, my tenacity to get through it, to see the light, my resilience and strength prevail. Rejection, abandonment, wanting to be liked and accepted. Finding my truth, my inner strength, and the love within me, it's been an incredible journey. To be bold AF. I'm not the one to stand loud and proud and to scream from the rooftop. I'm gentle and soft, yet honest and real. I'm proud of the woman I am today. I'm proud of my values and what I stand for. It's kind of miraculous to look back at my journey to see where I've travelled. To stand up and say this is me. I'm good. Love me or don't, it's okay either way.

There is much to be said with the inner work, our independent healing journey, but I also believe we need human connection—healthy, safe interactions—coregulation and that we heal through love and healthy relationships. I believe we are all on a soul journey. We chose to be here, and we have a reason for it. The people along our journey help us with our mission. Along the way, we experience lessons and blessings that help form and shape us. My wish for all of us is that we continue to find inner truth in our soul's mission. Find our voice with love, gratitude, forgiveness, and compassion for ourselves and for others. And may we all find love that creates safety, depth, and connections at the heart.

In May 2020, I created a profile on the dating app Her. For women looking to meet women. Reflecting on my experience in my 20s and the incredible connection we had, and the curiosity I played out in my head over the years. I am single, newly empowered with what I want to create for myself and in a relationship. My profile: confused and not sure what I want. My truth: embarrassed to declare my truths, what if someone I know saw me on this app? What would they think? Gulp. I chatted with a few women who were kind to share their stories of coming out later in life and some podcasts that I might find helpful. Then I met a friend. She flat out told me that I wasn't her type and that she felt compelled to warn me of the women out there who would try to take advantage of me. It became a safe exchange that quickly developed into flirtation and then an extraordinary bond of love.

My commitment to myself in venturing into this—at all costs, be real, authentic, and vulnerable. The love and partnership that has been birthed from this intent is magical. It takes work, and it gets uncomfortable. I have attempted to run away multiple times. I look for evidence on how or why it won't work. I can't see the vision of the future, and it drives me nuts—a struggle I have. But what I can see is the depth in connection it creates when I take risks and be vulnerable. The more I soften into who I am and the love that is between us. There are no coincidences in life. When the student is ready, the teacher will appear. In this case, quite literally.

Am I gay? Apparently that is quite obvious to others. For me, it's been a denial of labels. No one puts baby in the corner—and no one puts labels on her. Lol. I loved the man I married, and I love my girlfriend. For me, it's the connection, not the sorting label. The body parts are fun in their differing ways, but love is love. My daughter struggles with her parents not being together. Living a very hetero life, she also struggles that her mom is a lesbian. It's strange to say that. I don't know that I would call myself that, but I am certainly involved in some very lesbian behaviour. I think my struggle is the acceptance in the world. It is safer to be married to a man. It's not like you go around in the world declaring you are straight to everyone you meet, nor does it even matter. I want to feel safe. I want my kids, all kids, to feel safe. But not at the cost of self-expression and living our own truths.

I sometimes cringe when I think about my first post-separation intimate experience. I feel the embarrassment and shame still within me. No one will know him (thankfully!), but I knew the circumstances, and they were not in line with my values. I chased an illusion, something that didn't make a whole lot of sense but felt good in the moment on some level. To feel wanted, I suppose. I was caught up in the connection. I didn't have boundaries, and I didn't know how to say no. What I learned was priceless as I observed how I instinctively nurtured someone else's needs over my own values and then the cost that had on me, my heart.

The same thing happened when I had the affair. I knew better. But what I didn't know was how to hold space in a connection and not have it mean something about my life. How to not get swept up in the illusion of what was there. I truly had the awakening of my lack of happiness with myself and at home. For this, I have peace. I have forgiveness within me. I lived and learned.

What's not included in my story above are the experiences that tie into my fear of illness and the often present question, what is wrong with me. Our bodies speak to us in an attempt to show us what needs our attention. A cry for us to slow down, make a change or find some deep healing. It's a reframe to look at the symptoms we experience, not as the cause or something that is broken or failing us, but merely a sign to lead us to the root. Looking back with this awareness, I can see how my body has spoken to me through anxiety, depression, fatigue, various aches in my body, back pain that led to major surgery, rollercoaster of digestive flareups, joint pain (debilitating at times), constantly fighting colds, Raynaud's, sensitivities to food and the sun, insomnia, PMS, childhood asthma, chronic ear, and sinus infections, and injuries: broken bones, strains and sprains, and three concussions.

When we experience trauma, it creates toxic stress within the body that creates vulnerability and susceptibility to illness and disease.

Childhood trauma, even more so, has its lasting impact on our bodies as a result of cellular vulnerability during developmental stages. On top of this, we don't have a safe space to express emotions nor develop the skills to process them. The correlation of our internal emotional footprints or wounds directly ties to our wellbeing.

The stories above capture some of the big distress (or big 'T' trauma) that I faced over the years. But there are also the little 't' trauma events that happen in our lives. Seemingly small events can create the experience of trauma within. A recent example that I uncovered for myself was an incident when I was about five. I brushed by the confection stand at the grocery store checkout line, and a pack of gum fell to the floor. There were rules when inside the store: we did not touch anything, and we did not ask for anything. We behaved, and if we were lucky, we got a treat. As the gum hit the floor, I panicked. Scared for my life, I picked the gum up and put it in my pocket. During a recent healing session, I uncovered a truth within me. Almost 40 years later, I was still affected by this subconscious imprint 'I don't make good choices'. Healing this has allowed me to transform the part of me that is constantly questioning myself, agonizing over the idea of whether I made the right decision or not with everything.

Trauma is not what happens to you. Trauma is what happens inside you as a result of what happens to you. - Gabore Mate

---

For the past decade, I have been studying holistic sciences and healing, self-help, and mindset strategies. It began with a quest to find another option to the prognosis of medication for life coupled with the idea that most of what I was experiencing was all in my head. For years I craved that one course, one book, one supplement that would take it all away. I've now embraced the journey, the energetic expansion that comes after the contraction, the peeling back of the onion layers.

I've been blessed to be part of some miraculous life-transforming courses. Courses that have opened my eyes in ways I never imagined, have softened my heart, gifted me with incredible friendships with myself and with others, and have led me to the life I live today. All of this is priceless.

Here are some other things that I have found acceptance with.

- Intimacy, depth, and vulnerability are my jam. To experience it, I must be it
- To be intimate is to share me, to allow myself to be seen
- I'm socially awkward, and I am challenged with surface-level small talk
- Life is not linear, although societal expectations are
- My innate curiosity to know and understand how things work is a great asset
- I have so much love in my heart.
- I'm a big kid with a playful side that I share when I feel safe to do so
- I love to learn, especially around the transformation of health
- I will never just focus on one thing and will always take a multifaceted approach. A true Manifesting Generator

I am breaking free, opening up to my truths, finding my inner beauty and self-worth. It feels rather serendipitous to write, but there is a becoming of it that is quite beautiful—letting down my armour and finding and giving myself permission to own the feminine energy within me. To own the strength and courage that I have. I can accept myself. I'm committed to growth—to know and do better. For being the best version that I can be. Most of all, being an example for my kids.

I began to recognize that when I wanted something, I made it happen. I wanted a car, and I got one. I wanted to learn how to play hockey, so at 20, I taught myself to skate and learned to play. I declared that I would make $100k a year. That one took a little longer, but it happened. I wanted to meet a man with a list of great qualities, and I married that man. I wanted to be with a woman, I am. I wanted kids, and I am blessed with two. I wanted to go back to school to study osteopathy, and I'm in my 4th and final year. I wanted to find another solution to the prognosis of medication for life, and I became a Holistic Nutritionist and studied health and the emotional connection with such rigor and passion and changed my diet and lifestyle. I wanted intimacy and vulnerability in my life, and I now have incredible intimacy with my friends and partner. I wanted to heal and feel confident in myself and who I am so that I could be of service to others, I became a Tao Hands Practitioner, and an Emotional Freedom and Core Clearing Practitioner, and I am healing. I wanted to find my voice, and I am now an author.

2021 has been a year like no other. This past year my healing transformation was up levelled in astonishing ways with the combination of spiritual soulful healing, emotional healing and nutrition, and metabolic reset. At 43, I am more grounded, clear, and peaceful than ever. I am softening into my strengths. No longer on the run in the game of survival, but finding stillness in my knowing, my truths, and my values. With great challenge comes great gifts. Writing this chapter has been exactly that.

Loving ourselves through the process of owning our story is the bravest thing we will ever do

- *Brene Brown*

Mom, I know you're there. I know I've written things that might hurt. I'm sorry for any pain this may cause you. You are an incredible woman with so much strength. I know you may not see things like I do and that we may not share the same views. I now know that's okay. I hope you know that too. I love you like crazy and always will. Did you know that my name means strong and brave? I think it's quite fitting, wouldn't you say? Thank you for gifting me life.

Di, my little big sis, my rock, my greatest companion. Thank you for being my world in so many ways. I love you.

Jon, I will forever be grateful for our relationship and our time together. We had a lot of fun! Thank you for unintentionally cracking my heart open and showing me love. For holding space for me to grow into myself. Thank you for your strength. For being such an incredible dude, a real manly man. Thank you for our children and for trusting me on that adventure. You're an amazing dad. I'm sorry my lesson on acceptance didn't line up. I'm sorry for the hurt I caused you. Thank you for always standing in your truths and for always being there. I love you, always.

Megan, Thank you for saying yes to being my friend. Thank you for loving me the way you do and seeing me in ways that I am still opening up to. You are a gift, a blessing, and divine timing. Thank you for growing with me, for your generosity, for believing in me, and for always cheering me on. You're beautiful. I love you.

To my kids, thank you for choosing me to be your mom. Thank you for your love, your sensitive souls, your kindness, and your laughter. You are my favourite.

Karl, my unsung hero. There are no words to describe my gratitude for you and your incredible heart. Thank you for being an angel. I love you.

To everyone else I know. Thank you for your impact on my life, big or small. Don't ever question your importance to me. I love you.

For the strangers I have yet to meet. Thank you for reading my story. I appreciate you.

ABOUT THE AUTHOR

VALERIE SMITH

Valerie Smith, an Integrative Healer, and lifelong learner. A passionate advocate for healthy living, natural solutions, and creating safe spaces for intimacy and vulnerability that lead to growth and healing.

On her personal quest for healing, coupled with an innate curiosity to understand the human body, Valerie has been studying holistic health sciences for over a decade from both eastern and western philosophies to address the physical, mental, emotional, and spiritual body and the interconnectedness. Val is a Holistic Nutritionist, Metabolic Balance Coach, Tao Hands Practitioner, Thai Massage Practitioner, and an Emotional Freedom Technique (EFT) and Core Clearing Practitioner and is in her 4th and final year studying to become a Manual Osteopath.

Val takes a no-nonsense approach to creating optimum health for herself and her clients. With a passion for understanding the root cause, including emotional blockages and patterns of behaviour that keep you stuck. Filled with compassion, a deep desire to make a difference, and the drive for you to achieve the results you're looking for.

Val is on a mission to help others transform their health, to guide them through their healing journey, and empower them with lifelong strategies for ultimate success.

Give yourself the gift of healing—it's within you.

Connect with Valerie
Website: www.valeriesmith.ca

ABOUT THE PUBLISHER

SOULFULLY ALIGNED PUBLISHING HOUSE

*S*oulfully Aligned Publishing House exists to bring healing, transformation and aligned service through the written word to the world.

Created and founded by Best Selling Author, Sandra Rodriguez Bicknell and Vanessa Ferraro, their mission is to highlight the voices of healers around the world to the mainstream to exemplify the power of having a story, and not being your story. Soulfully Aligned Publishing donates all book proceeds to various charities around the world as chosen by their authors. We are committed to bringing conscious, harmonious principles to the way we operate our business and are here to magnify and empower all whom we work with to align to their Soul, their message and their service to the world.

Printed in Great Britain
by Amazon

77158294R00093